William Henry King

The Situation in Cuba

William Henry King

The Situation in Cuba

ISBN/EAN: 9783337379193

Printed in Europe, USA, Canada, Australia, Japan

Cover: Foto ©ninafisch / pixelio.de

More available books at **www.hansebooks.com**

THE SITUATION IN CUBA.

SPEECH

OF

HON. WILLIAM H. KING,

OF UTAH,

IN THE

HOUSE OF REPRESENTATIVES,

Thursday, January 20, 1898.

WASHINGTON.

1898.

SPEECH

OF

HON. WILLIAM H. KING.

The House being in Committee of the Whole on the state of the Union, and having under consideration the bill (H. R. 6419) making appropriations for the diplomatic and consular service for the fiscal year ending June 30, 1899—

Mr. KING said:

Mr. CHAIRMAN: Yesterday the distinguished chairman of the Committee on Foreign Affairs [Mr. HITT] presented certain phases of the Cuban question. It is known that during the entire period of the extra session members upon this side of the House were endeavoring to secure not only a discussion of this question, but some action which would be the contribution of at least moral aid to the Cuban insurgents struggling so heroically for freedom. But the rules of the House forbade discussion, and the other side of the Chamber pursued a course of inexplicable silence. We were powerless. Though representatives of a free people, freedom of speech was denied in this representative body. While we were meeting every third day, merely for the purpose of enabling the majority to compel an adjournment, it was known that starvation and death and the most frightful devastation were decimating the most beautiful island of the sea. We knew that Weyler was butchering and destroying, that the greatest crime of the century was being committed, and yet we uttered no protest, we sent no word of cheer to those who so bravely had withstood the assaults of the greatest armies that had ever crossed the mighty deep.

Immediately after convening in December last, efforts were again made to secure consideration of this burning question. Since last May a resolution, passed by the Senate and which accorded the Cuban insurgents the rights of belligerency, has been lying upon the Speaker's table and in some quiet recess provided by the chairman of the Committee on Foreign Affairs; and the demands of the Democrats of the House and of the people of the United States had proven unavailing to bring it forth into the light.

We were impotent to discharge a solemn obligation and perform a national duty. It is not my purpose to inveigh against the rules of this House or indulge in denunciation of any persons or party, but to concisely and as plainly as possible state the facts relating to the Cuban question. After three years of sanguinary struggles, during all of which time the peace of our nation has been disturbed and the interests of our citizens seriously affected, neither the Administration nor the party controlling legislation offers any solution of the question.

I listened in vain when the gentleman from Illinois [Mr. HITT] was speaking, hoping that some proposition would be suggested indicative of a determination upon the part of the party in power to wisely and heroically deal with the situation which the Cuban question presents. His speech was barren upon this matter; but

2   3223

it was an eloquent appeal for nonaction upon the part of this Congress.

It was a plea for further confidence in Spain and Spanish methods, yet replete with confessions, more or less disguised, of Spain's indefensible treatment of Cuba and her inability to reassert her authority in her lost province. His appeal for all patriotic Americans to support the President in whatever steps were necessary for the vindication of the honor and the protection of the interests of our country, found sympathetic auditors upon this side of the Chamber.

It is unnecessary to assure the gentleman that in every emergency and in every hour of peril, our hands and hearts will as loyally uphold the integrity and honor of our nation, as the distinguished gentleman and his political associates. And any criticisms which we offer, are predicated upon the statement that the Administration, and gentlemen on the other side of the Chamber, have omitted to vindicate the rights of our Government and to patriotically pursue a national policy which has become a positive national duty.

We sincerely invite our Republican friends to an immediate performance of long-neglected responsibilities, to bring from the committee's table the resolution according belligerent rights to the followers of the Cuban Republic, and to inaugurate a foreign policy that will establish peace in Cuba and terminate, to use the words of my eloquent friend from Illinois, " the troubles, the confusions, the destructions, and the hopeless condition of things in the island so adjacent to our shores."

He will find every Democrat in this House supporting him, and the Administration in such a course, so in consonance with the desires of the American people and so essential to be pursued in order to maintain the honor and dignity of the United States. The gentleman's words are not reassuring; they are not harbingers of peace. Indeed, they are followed with lamentations and portend impending dangers. Hopeful of peace, they are prophetic of international complications which may result in war.

But permeating his speech, through and through, is the anxiously expressed, and unexpressed, desire that the threatening clouds may be dissipated. If a wise and statesmanlike policy had been pursued, there would have been no overhanging clouds to disquiet us, and the glorious sun of Cuban liberty would now be radiating its brightness upon us. And even now, if the President will join us in immediately recognizing the Cuban insurgents as entitled to all the rights of belligerents, our nation, without contest with Spain or any departure from that high plane of moral, national, and international duty which it should pursue under all circumstances, will soon witness Cuba's emancipation from the imperialism of Spain, and behold her clothed in all the splendor of a free and independent nation.

Why procrastinate? Why await the action of the Executive? In the language of the distinguished gentleman [Mr. HITT] while speaking of the action of this body when passing a belligerency resolution at the time Mr. Cleveland was President, "this House is impatient of the apathy of the Executive of the United States." Any action upon the part of this Government that will give the insurgents the status of a nation requires the action of Congress.

I occupy, perhaps, different ground from some of the gentlemen upon this side of the House in believing that the hour has arrived for intervention upon the part of this Government to prevent the

3223

complete devastation of Cuba and the continuation of the internecine struggle which will only result in the further destruction of thousands of innocent women and children and the ultimate expulsion of the armies and authority of Spain from the blood-soaked island. That course may mean war with Spain, but it will prevent Spain from starving 200,000 more helpless people now herded by her soldiers and in a decisive manner terminate the contest which, without such proceeding, may continue indefinitely.

However, there can be no defense for refusing the course first suggested. Last May, when the Senate by resolution recognized the insurgents as belligerents, this House ought to have immediately passed the resolution and the Executive ought to have concurred therein. With the advantages which would have followed, it must be apparent to all that Cuba's independence would long since have been achieved. The refusal of this House to pass the resolution was cowardly and indefensible. By so doing we have contributed to Spanish supremacy and have been Spain's potential ally in the unequal contest. We have aided her in making of Cuba a charnel house.

By this crime of omission we have enabled her to kill by starvation hundreds of thousands of reconcentrados. Instead of assuming the position of strict neutrality, we have acted as prochien ami to Spain. And now we are told to wait, and to hesitate, and to let the work of starvation and death continue. The conduct of Spain the distinguished gentleman characterizes as "barbarous and a war of extermination." If so, why condone and defend it? Why contribute to the barbarity and extermination by refusing moral aid to the insurgents? Do not stronger reasons now exist for declaring the contest between the Cubans and the Spanish a civil war than were found two years ago, when, by resolution earnestly supported by the gentleman from Illinois and his party, it was stated that a "condition of war existed in Cuba"?

The revolution then had been in progress but a year. Now three years have elapsed. The civil government of the revolutionists had not then fully demonstrated its undisputed control over the military organization. Indubitable proof in rich abundance is known now to us all, of the stability of the civil power, of the orderly conduct of all civil and administrative functions, of the Cuban Republic, and of the complete dependency of the military organization upon the civil power.

In 1896 the universality of the Cuban sentiment against Spain was not so conspicuous as now. It was then claimed that the supporters of the revolutionary movement were few in number; that they lacked coherency and that patriotic impulse which would bind them into homogeneous action. It is now conclusively demonstrated that the Cuban people en masse are revolutionists; that they are possessed of a fixed determination to wrest their independence from the absolutism of Spain, and that whether in the field fighting under the Cuban flag, or pursuing as best they may, in the cities and towns, the peaceful arts, they are all bound together by purposes and designs stronger than links of steel, and do not hesitate to declare that they have consecrated their fortunes and their lives upon freedom's altar.

Two years ago there was room for doubt as to the ability of the Cubans to continue the contest. The unconquered courage of the mighty Canovas, whose words, "The last dollar and the last man," had aroused Spain to the most gigantic efforts, and had

3223

laden the sea with ships and sails bearing the mightiest army ever
sent to the New World. Would the revolutionary forces, lacking
discipline, without arms or military equipments, be able to with-
stand the assaults of Spain's unnumbered hosts? That question
had received no answer then. Now we know that the armies of
Spain have melted away, while the insurgents are better disciplined, armed, and equipped than ever before.

The past two years have only strengthened the revolutionists.
Spain has grown weaker. Her resources are exhausted; her grasp
upon the island is relaxing; yet with a death-like struggle she
clings tenaciously, preferring the destruction of the island, the
death of its people, her own impoverishment, and the blood of her
children, conscripted from the beautiful valleys of her empire, to
the relinquishment of a claim founded upon discovery, and which
the judgment of the world pronounces invalid because of oppression and tyranny.

The eminent gentleman from Pennsylvania [Mr. ADAMS], who
has just addressed the committee, animadverted upon the conduct
of Mr. Cleveland while President, and seemed to deduce therefrom
the idea that the Democrats of the House are not sincere in their
advocacy of Cuba's cause. I desire to state that Mr. Cleveland did
not, in dealing with the Cuban question, represent the wishes of
the Democratic party.

Mr. Cleveland at that time had ceased to be a Democrat. Neither upon the financial question nor upon many others was he
in harmony with his party. He was repudiated at the national
convention at Chicago. The only supporters of his financial policy
and the only sharers of many of his political views are to be found
in the ranks of those who supported the present Executive of the
United States in the last election. So my criticisms of the deal-
ings of this Government with the Cuban question are not confined
to that period covered by the Administration of Mr. McKinley.

During the incumbency of Mr. Cleveland, when Americans
were incarcerated and when Spain was proceeding in a high-
handed manner in dealing with American interests, both Mr.
Cleveland and Mr. Olney were derelict in their duty and failed to
give that support to Consul-General Lee which that brave official
deserved and which the interests of American citizens demanded.
However, it seems from the message of President Cleveland, com-
municated December 7, 1896, that he had reached the conclusion
that the policy of nonintervention could not much longer be followed. These words are significant:

It should be added that it can not be reasonably assumed that the hitherto
expectant attitude of the United States will be indefinitely maintained.
While we are anxious to accord all due respect to the sovereignty of Spain,
we can not view the pending conflict in all its features and properly apprehend our inevitably close relations to it and its possible results without considering that by the course of events we may be drawn into such an unusual
and unprecedented condition as will fix a limit to our patient waiting for
Spain to end the contest, either alone and in her own way, or with our
friendly cooperation.

When the inability of Spain to deal successfully with the insurrection has
become manifest and it is demonstrated that her sovereignty is extinct in
Cuba for all purposes of its rightful existence, and when a hopeless struggle
for its reestablishment has degenerated into a strife which means nothing
more than the useless sacrifice of human life and the utter destruction of the
very subject-matter of the conflict, a situation will be presented in which
our obligations to the sovereignty of Spain will be superseded by higher
obligations which we can hardly hesitate to recognize and discharge.

Even at that time the observance of the unequivocal meaning
of these robust words would have required immediate action upon

3223

the part of the Government looking to a cessation of the fratricidal struggle so horrifying to the American people and to the entire world. It was then well understood that Spain's sovereignty was extinct in Cuba not only for all purposes of "its rightful existence," but for any purpose whatever, and that the warfare conducted had "degenerated into a strife which was neither more nor less than the useless sacrifice of human life" and the utter destruction of the island and its people, "the very subject-matter of the conflict."

But the attitude of the Republicans in the House during the past eight months becomes still more unfathomable when we consider that portion of their platform adopted at St. Louis which refers to this subject. It is there declared that—

The Government of Spain having lost control of Cuba, and being unable to protect the property or lives of resident American citizens or to comply with its treaty obligations, we believe that the Government of the United States should actively use its influence and good offices to restore peace and give independence to the island.

This declaration has been flagrantly and deliberately violated by the party adopting it, and ignored, if not repudiated, by the President whose nomination was based upon the platform containing it. If in June, 1896, when this platform was adopted, the Government of Spain had "lost control of Cuba," were not the evidences more manifold in May, 1897, at which time Democrats, while gagged and bound by the majority in the House, insisted that our voices should be lifted in behalf of the Cuban Republic?

Have not intervening events exemplified the wisdom of that platform utterance, and does not the hour now demand that that promise should be fulfilled? Not a single word has been uttered in the House by the party in power in harmony with the statement just referred to. If the Government of the United States in 1896 should have actively used its influence to restore peace and give independence to Cuba, why not now? Or if our friends controlling the Government admit this course to be radical, why not grant belligerent rights?

Do they desire the independence of Cuba? If so, give to the insurgents a national status, the right to float their flag upon the high seas, to enter our ports and claim the rights of neutrals—in a word, recognize them as belligerents. This ought not to be a party question. There should be no aisle between us when Cuba lies prostrate. The cause of liberty and humanity should be as dear to the gentlemen upon the other side of the House as to those sitting near me.

That policy which condemns our Government to isolation is not to be commended. Nations are but individuals, and the law which governs an individual in all its moral phases should control the nation. Sympathy for oppression, altruism working for a brighter and happier day, exemplified faith seeking in darkness and uncertainty the dawn of freedom's day, wherein the highest achievements and perfections of heart and brain are possible—these are the seeds planted within us all to blossom and flower and bring full fruition.

And so every effort to stand in that brighter day should be encouraged and not disfavored. Moreover, this nation stands as the archetype to the world. When despots tremble at threatened revolutions occasioned by their tyranny, and adopt repressive measures to prevent the consummation of the people's will, we rejoice at their discomfiture, and earnestly desire that the blessings we enjoy shall extend to the oppressed and downtrodden.

3223

The people of the United States expect, and they have a right to expect, that their servants in Congress will give expression, by legislation where needed, to the views and sentiments which they so strongly entertain. Not for a moment during the present struggle in Cuba have the American people abated their interest in this momentous controversy; nor have they doubted the course which this Government ought to pursue. There has been no discordant note from them. They have declared over and over again in favor of belligerency for the patriotic Cubans. The only harsh voice has come from the moneyed interests, the stock brokers, the coupon clippers, the representatives of capital, and the commercial interests. But thus it ever was.

Commercialism and the bloodless form of wealth never know country or friend or liberty. They outlaw themselves from humanity, and become forever the enemies to freedom's cause. When Grant desired the freedom of Cuba during the ten years' war, Wall street, speaking through Hamilton Fish, prevented that great man from carrying into effect the purpose born of his noble heart. Liberty creates wealth, because it destroys discriminations, proscriptions, and favored legislation (which crush the many to enrich the few), and opens the broad, wide avenues of human endeavor equally to all the children of men.

But wealth, much of which is the very child of liberty, becomes her foe and compasses her destruction. The cruel, heartless power of wealth controls nations and policies to-day. It declares war and compels peace. It fashions legislation, and dominates kings and potentates, ministers and legislative bodies. It is a "sordid despotism," macadamizing the pathway of life with human bones cemented with human blood. It placed the armies of England in the land of the pyramids as taskmasters and tax-gatherers for the bondholders of Europe. It wrung by oppressive, unjust taxation more than $26,000,000 annually from Cuba's impoverished children. It covers Cuba with its bonds and insolently demands that this nation shall take no step which may strengthen the purpose of the Cuban army to throw off the grinding tyranny under which the Cuban people have labored.

When we would lift our hand to do the right, it is palsied by wealth; and when our tongues would speak for Cuba's liberty, stock jobbers and bondholders bid them be silent, and our lips are sealed. Let us invoke the spirit of liberty, and conjure from the past those immortal forms that will enable us to break the spell now binding us, that we may do our duty, not only to our brothers who fight in freedom's holy cause, but to ourselves, our country, and those who shall come after us. Who gave man the right to chain the human mind and to bond islands and nations and to oppress his brother? Governments rightly exist only when they derive their just powers from the consent of the governed.

Let us reread the Declaration of Independence and have it interpreted, not by Wall street, not by French bondholders, but construed by the inspiration of freedom's undying spirit. We do not want war if it can be avoided consistent with duty and honor. Even at this late hour all conflict may be escaped if belligerent rights are given to the Cubans. Neither is it desired that we shall regard lightly treaties and protocols and national obligations. A code of honor should prevail among nations as among individuals; but because of treaty stipulations with Spain, we are not to be constrained from expressing disapproval of her barbarous, cruel, inhuman, rapacious conduct, and the nameless atrocities committed by her against her own children as well as American citizens.

Neither national nor international law requires this; nor is it violative of treaty obligations, where there is a revolt against the titular government, to assume the attitude of neutrality between the parent and the contending child. Nay, it is a duty (where exist wrongs so long endured as to compel revolution) to at least recognize a state of war and accord belligerent rights. Because of the anxiety of the Democratic party to avert war, we desire that belligerent rights shall be granted the insurgents. And I have no hesitation in stating that if this uncertain, halting, hopeless, purposeless, objectless policy now being pursued by the Administration shall be continued, complications will arise and difficulties accumulate until war will be inevitable if the honor and dignity of this Government shall be preserved. A few moments ago I called attention to the fact that stronger reasons existed to-day for action upon our part than prevailed when the House and Senate passed a resolution in 1896 recognizing the belligerency of the Cuban people. I desire to quote from statements made by distinguished Republicans when the resolution was under consideration.

On the 5th day of February, 1896, the following resolution was introduced in the Senate:

Resolved by the Senate (the House of Representatives concurring), That in the opinion of Congress a condition of public war exists between the Government of Spain and the government proclaimed and for some time maintained by force of arms by the people of Cuba, and that the United States of America should maintain a strict neutrality between the contending powers, according to each all the rights of belligerents in the ports and territory of the United States. To which was added, February 28, the following:

Resolved further, That the friendly offices of the United States should be offered by the President to the Spanish Government for the recognition of the independence of Cuba.

This resolution was reported by the Committee on Foreign Relations, of which the present Secretary of State, Mr. Sherman, was chairman. In advocating the adoption of the resolution, that distinguished gentleman said:

In every aspect in which I can look at this matter it seems to me that this comparatively ignorant, comparatively inoffensive population, composed of native Cubans, emancipated blacks, and free mulattoes, have, in their victory over greater numbers, acquired the position of belligerents.

The gentleman went even further than the resolution called for. He stated:

My convictions are strong, made stronger every day, that the condition of affairs in Cuba is such that the intervention of the United States must sooner or later be given to put an end to the crimes that are almost beyond description.

Speaking of the conduct of Weyler and the course which that Spanish general proposed to pursue, the eminent gentleman from Ohio said:

I wish to say, upon my own responsibility, that if this line of conduct is pursued by Spain in Cuba and the people of the United States are informed of its conditions as they are narrated daily in the public papers, there is no earthly power that will prevent the people of the United States from going over to that island and running all over its length and breadth and driving out from the little Island of Cuba these barbarous robbers and imitators of the worst men who ever lived in the world.

Concluding his powerful speech, the gentleman said:

Sir, whatever may be the result of the adoption of this measure, I desire to take my share of responsibility in connection with it, and with a confidence in the judgment of the Almighty Ruler of the Universe, I believe it is wise if we can assist, and bid the other nations of the world concur, in securing for the people of Cuba the same liberties we now enjoy.

3223

These statements, when placed in contrast with the silence of the Secretary of State during the past eight months, can not but provoke comment. As Senator he was willing to grant belligerency as early as February 28, 1896. Now, after more battles have been won and the permanency of the Cuban Republic is assured, after Spain's barbarity has been more clearly seen and Weyler's " proposed policy " has become a realized fact, we hear nothing from the distinguished gentleman from which it may be inferred that these views are still maintained by him. On February 11, 1870, so fully imbued was the distinguished gentleman with the idea that a state of war existed in Cuba that he introduced a resolution in the Senate of the United States which reads as follows:

Whereas the United States observe with deep interest the cruel war now existing in Cuba and sympathize with its people, as with the people of all American nations or colonies in their efforts to secure independence of European power: Therefore,

Be it resolved, etc., That the United States recognize the present existence of a state of war between the Kingdom of Spain and the country of Cuba, waged upon the part of Cuba to establish its independence, and that the United States will observe strict neutrality between the belligerent parties as to their duty under the law of nations.

If we remember the situation of the Cuban revolutionists in 1870, it is incomprehensible that there should be opposition now to the adoption of a similar resolution. In 1870 there were less than 10,000 insurgents in the field. Their operations were confined exclusively to the eastern provinces of the island. There was scarcely a semblance of civil authority. Spain's possession of the island was almost complete and her dominion but little weakened; yet the then Senator from Ohio [Mr. Sherman], distinguished for his ability and knowledge of international law, felt that the revolutionists were entitled to belligerency.

The resolution first quoted passed the Senate February 28, 1896, 64 votes being in favor of it and only 6 against it. Among the eminent Republicans voting for the resolution were Senators CULLOM, ELKINS, FRYE, LODGE, PROCTOR, Sherman, and THURSTON. On March 2, 1896, the present chairman of the Committee on Foreign Affairs of the House [Mr. HITT] reported the following resolution and moved its adoption as a substitute for the one which had passed the Senate:

Resolved, That in the opinion of Congress a state of public war exists in Cuba, the parties to which are entitled to belligerent rights, and the United States should observe a strict neutrality between the belligerents.

Resolved, That Congress deplores the destruction of life and property caused by the war now waging in that island, and believing that the only permanent solution of the contest equally in the interest of Spain, the people of Cuba, and the other nations would be in the establishment of a government by the choice of the people of Cuba, it is the sense of Congress that the Government of the United States should use its good offices and friendly influences to that end.

Resolved, That the United States has not intervened in struggles between any European Governments and their colonies on this continent; but from the very close relations between the people of the United States and those of Cuba, in consequence of its proximity and the extent of the commerce between the two peoples, the present war is entailing such losses upon the people of the United States that Congress is of the opinion that the Government of the United States should be prepared to protect the legitimate interests of our citizens by intervention, if necessary.

The chairman of the committee, speaking to the substitute, stated:

Mr. Speaker, the resolutions presented to the House at this moment have been considered with great care by the committee of the House specially charged with that duty. In many meetings, through several months, the question involved has been discussed. These resolutions have been ripened and matured after consultation with the most eminent jurists; and it is believed that in the interest of right, in the interest of peace, in the interest of our own country, and in the interest of those elsewhere who are making a struggle with which we sympathize, these resolutions present the most practical, conservative, and effective mode of action and expression by Congress.

Further on in his speech he used the following language:

All these resolutions, Mr. Speaker, that have been offered by the Committee on Foreign Affairs, and the terms in which they have been stated, have been carefully considered, so that we believe they can not, and certainly ought not to, cause any trouble or rupture between us and any country that is not seeking trouble with us. * * * First, as to the belligerency of the Cubans, if that is a fact and truth, we may recognize it; if it is not—if it is a falsehood—we ought not to recognize it under any circumstances. Now, let us see what are the facts. That there is a state of war—that there is belligerency—can hardly be denied in view of the overwhelming evidence of a state of war.

The distinguished gentleman then fortified this statement, as well as the resolution declaring the existence of a state of public war in Cuba, by referring not only to the newspaper reports, but to the official consular reports "lying before the members of the House for weeks." Reference is further made to the statement of American consuls that the armed forces of the insurgents, "contending with desperate earnestness and unconquered will," were "three times" greater than those engaged in the rebellion between 1868 and 1878. He conclusively demonstrated the existence of war in Cuba, and, as evidence, cited the tremendous efforts being put forth by Spain to overcome the insurrection.

Other gentlemen, who are now silent when we seek the passage of a similar resolution, eloquently contended that a state of war existed in Cuba, and that it was the duty of this Government to accord belligerent rights to the struggling patriots. In closing the debate on March 2, 1896, the distinguished chairman [Mr. HITT], in reply to arguments which had been made against the resolution, stated:

Nearly six months ago the official reports that lie before me show that there were 35,000 men in arms defending that insurgent government organization, which is a power. Armed forces, not altogether a government according to the notions of some nice lawyers, but a great armed political movement, as Wheaton says, has been formed, a powerful movement, which is belligerent, which is war, and which is entitled to recognition. The gentleman spoke of the apprehension that it would bring on speedy hostilities. If he reads the resolution with care he will see what is the opinion of men whose province it is to deal with this question that there is no ground to apprehend that they will be received in such a spirit, for they plainly are not meant in such terms. They are a distinct vindication of our rights; they are the expression of our duties.

How the position then taken by the gentleman can be reconciled with the one he now occupies must be left for his determination. All that was then said in justification of the resolution can now be declared, and much more can be urged. If a state of public war existed in Cuba then, certainly after nearly two years have passed, during which time the revolutionary forces have won repeated victories and the armies of Spain have been decimated and reduced to less than 60,000, the existence of war can not be denied.

The resolution, as shown by the CONGRESSIONAL RECORD of March 2, 1896, passed the House by a vote of 262 to 17. Owing to the disagreement of the two Houses upon the language of the resolutions, the matter was referred to a conference committee. The distinguished gentleman from Illinois was one of the conferees upon the part of the House and the present Secretary of State, Mr. Sherman, was one of the conferees upon the part of the Senate. After prolonged discussion the resolution which first passed the Senate was agreed to by the House.

3223

In urging the House to accept the Senate resolution the gentleman made an elaborate argument in favor of the belligerency of the insurgents, showing the forces which they had, the character of civil government, and the advantages which would result to them from the passage of the resolution. He stated that—

The Government of the insurgent movement, the revolution in Cuba, is a republican government with a president. * * * They have an organization of civil officers. They have secured possession of province after province. In some cases they have almost all of the territory of a province in peaceful occupation administered by their officers. * * *

They have shown all these high qualities and done all these great deeds without the sordid hope of reward, bearing themselves more patiently through this incessant struggle than our fathers did during the saddest period of the Revolutionary war. * * * It is our duty to pass these resolutions. These people are imitating us. All the traditions of Americans, all our past, everything in our own history appeals to us to cheer and encourage rather than aid to trample upon these men in Cuba who are struggling to become what we are. The House by an overwhelming vote passed the Senate resolutions. And so far as the legislative department of the Government had authority, belligerent rights were accorded the insurgents.

The action of President Cleveland in respect to the matter deserves the severest condemnation. If he had performed his duty, the Cuban question would have been a matter of history and would no longer have concerned us. In view of the record just referred to, I am at a loss to understand the quiescent attitude of our Republican friends and their determination to prevent discussion of or action upon the resolution now before the Committee on Foreign Relations. It is true the recent message of the President, as well as the statement of the distinguished gentleman from Illinois, attempts to supply a reason for the policy of the Administration.

It is argued that such changes have recently occurred in the administration by Spain of Cuban affairs as to forbid the taking of any step by this Government which might be construed as hostile to the Spanish Government. The overthrow of the Conservative party in Spain, the accession of Sagasta to power, and the promulgation of his autonomistic scheme for Cuba, are assigned as grounds for a reversal of the course of Congress two years ago, and an adherence to the present policy of inaction and nonintervention. It is also urged that General Weyler has been recalled and that General Blanco, who has succeeded him, is pursuing such a humane policy that it would be an evidence of unfriendliness upon our part to grant belligerent rights to the insurgents. None of the reasons assigned rests upon a substantial foundation. No change has occurred in Cuba and in the situation sufficient to restrain this Government from immediate action.

It is charitable to suppose that loyalty to the President impels Republicans to adhere to the policy now pursued, notwithstanding its variance from the plan heretofore advocated by them. The message of the President, relating to the Cuban situation, as well as the speech of the gentleman from Illinois [Mr. HITT], is erroneous, not only in its statement of facts, but its discussion of legal principles as applied to the question of belligerency, and the conclusions derived therefrom. The President declares (1) that he regards "the recognition of the belligerency of the Cuban insurgents as now unwise, and therefore inadmissible."

As justification for this view, he argues that the insurrection lacks those essential qualifications and is devoid of those characteristics, of that political organization, with the forms and functions of an ordinary government, which are indispensable to the recognition of belligerency. (2) He further contends that Sagasta's

Government has entered upon the work of administrative and political reforms which will give local self-government to the Cuban people; that it has not only recalled "the commander whose brutal orders inflamed the American mind and shocked the civilized world," but has accomplished such changes in the condition that time should be given to witness the evolution of peace and the pacification promised.

It is my purpose now to consider the second objection or point made by the President, reserving the discussion of the first one to a later period in my remarks.

It has been but a few days since my return from Cuba, and many members have requested me to explain the situation there, the condition of the people, the views of the Cubans, the progress of the war, and especially the changes, if any, wrought by Blanco and the autonomistic plan of the Spanish ministry.

In obedience to these requests and in order that the House may become cognizant of the facts that came to my knowledge while there, I will plainly state the result of my observations, averring preliminarily that there has been no such improvement as suggested by the President, and nothing whatever to occasion any delay upon the part of the United States in dealing with the question, or to lead to a belief that a "righteous peace is likely to be attained."

My visit to Cuba was entirely disinterested and for the sole purpose of learning something of a subject so transcendently important to the American people. I traveled extensively in the island, visiting four of the provinces and making personal investigations in scores of the cities and towns. Every opportunity was afforded me by General Blanco and other officials to see the people and observe the conditions prevailing. Everywhere the greatest kindness was manifested, and the various governors, alcaldes, civil and military authorities were sedulous in their attentions.

General Blanco and the general secretary, Dr. Congosto, stated fully their views of the situation, expressing gratification at the prospects of a speedy termination of all troubles and a successful implantation of autonomy in the affections of the people. Marquis Montero, Señor Galvez, and Dr. Zayas, members of the autonomistic cabinet, were no less enthusiastic in proclaiming the beauties of autonomy and the beneficial results soon to be realized from its establishment.

I met the leading autonomists from all parts of Cuba: prominent Spaniards and conservatives favored me with their views. I met and mingled with representatives from all parties, and persons from all vocations of life. The Spanish general, arrogant and proud, explained what was necessary in order to crush the revolutionary forces. The Spanish soldier told of his privations and regarded with unconcern the developments of the future.

Cuba to-day is almost indescribable. A reproduction of the scenes and sorrows there observable, a true recital of what has occurred and is daily transpiring, would arouse to immediate action the people of this great nation. This Congress would not dare to trifle with them and this question as it has during the past year.

Columbus, in describing Cuba, said:

Of all the lands, this is the most beautiful ever beheld by human eyes.

Such was Cuba, and such would Cuba be had the flag of Spain never floated over her soil. Spain's dominion has always corroded and poisoned. She has been a curse and scourge to the peoples of

323

two continents. Boasting of her Christianity and civilization, her treatment of conquered peoples has been so barbarous as to shock all nations. When her soldiers sacked a French colony and executed the entire garrison, they placed above their heads the words, "Not as Frenchmen, but as heretics."

In retaliation French soldiers captured a Spanish fort and hanged its defenders. Above them were written the words, "Not as Spaniards, but as murderers." Such an epitaph could justly be placed over the form of Spain's departed greatness and power in Cuba and in the New World. It will be remembered that upon Weyler's recall Spain authoritatively announced that pacification was complete in the provinces of Pinar del Rio, Habana, Matanzas, and Santa Clara, and that so successfully had been the military operations in the two eastern provinces that within a short period the revolution would terminate in the establishment of an honorable and perpetual peace.

But it was then known, not only to Spain but to all inquirers, that in the Provinces of Santiago de Cuba and Puerto Principe the insurgents were supreme, and that in the remaining provinces Spain's authority was limited to the fortified cities and towns. It was apparent that the policy of extermination pursued by Weyler had utterly failed to break the revolution and bring the Cuban people back to Spanish allegiance. To avert the impending tide of American indignation and prevent the interposition by this Government, Sagasta deftly offered the plan of autonomy.

This was the last arrow in Spain's quiver. It has been shot and has fallen short of its mark. It has failed, as it deserved to fail, because it was insincere and not designed to give the essentials of local self-government to the people of Cuba. It is a delusion and a sham. All shams sooner or later fail. The gentleman from Illinois contends that it is liberal and possesses the same characteristics found in Canada's organic law. The distinguished gentleman is certainly in error. Autonomy, as Sagasta said in proclaiming it, "affirms and strengthens the bond of sovereignty. In nothing is the central authority [Spain] diminished or weakened."

It is merely a coup de théâtre, and a fraudulent fabric suddenly evolved and offered to cheat the insurgents into laying down their arms, and to delude the American people into a policy of inaction. It is one of Spain's frequent coup d'états and pronunciamentos. It is an exemplification of her past policies of vice versa, of eternal promises to redress wrongs while secretly plotting to prevent the execution of reforms.

A careful examination of Sagasta's pronunciamento reveals its hypocrisy. The control of the subject of tariff and customs is of paramount importance to Cuba, and the imposition of unfriendly legislation in this direction disastrously affects the island; yet this subject, as provided in Sagasta's paper decree, he has so guarded and protected as to subserve entirely the interests of Spain, though grotesque attempts are made to conceal the unmistakable designs and unerring results. The peninsular government is permitted a differential tariff rate or duty of 35 per cent. This means that Cuba is still to be exploited in the interest of Spanish merchants, producers, and manufacturers.

To illustrate this feature and its extreme advantage to Spain: Suppose a rate of 10 per cent ad valorem were fixed as the duty on boots and shoes. Under the autonomistic plan Spain has the right to augment this by 35 per cent, so that all boots and shoes imported into Cuba from Spain would pay a 10 per cent duty only, while similar importations from all other countries would be required to pay a duty of 45 per cent. This discrimination is to compel Cuba to purchase from Spain—to sell in a cheap market and to buy in Spain's dear market.

Even if autonomy were genuine in all other respects, such a power as this with respect to its foreign commerce, placed in the hands of unfriendly ministers in Spain, could be made the engine of most fearful oppression, preventing Cuba's industrial and financial development and keeping her plundered for the enrichment of Spain's producers. But this is not all. The preparation of all schedules of duties is committed to a commission composed of insular and peninsular members of the Cortes, but with the ultimate power of control in the hands of the peninsular representatives.

The provision is that the commission shall be constituted of equal members selected from Spanish and Cuban representatives in the Cortes. All disagreements upon schedules or rates are to be determined by the senior member of the commission. Inasmuch as the selection of the representatives is largely under Spain's control, and remembering that from the members Cuba may have in the Cortes, some will belong to the Spanish party, it does not require remarkable prescience to foretell what the result will be.

The oldest member in the Cortes from Spain will be placed upon the commission. If all of the members of the commission from Cuba should be devoted to their country's interests and refuse consent to the tariff plan presented by Spain's commissioners, even then, with the senior member having the casting vote, which is tantamount to absolute control. the interests of the island would be sacrificed, and the original tariff schedule would be prepared in the interest of Spain.

Even if autonomy were to be successfully established, when it is attempted to put into execution the system of tariff taxation provided, such discords will arise as will inevitably produce civil war. Cuba's prosperity is dependent upon unrestricted commerce. Impediments such as Spain would interpose would immediately create stagnation, arrest industrial development, and the hardships thereby occasioned would be followed by mutterings and riots, which in turn would be succeeded by insurrections. and the grave of the past would be opened and the horrors of another sanguinary struggle be upon us.

But another feature more iniquitous than this is preserved in the proposed plan. The governor-general, appointed by the Crown, is made supreme. He can declare martial law, suspend the local assembly, veto its legislation, abrogate all civil guaranties, control all officials, and without restraint dispose of all offices. He may initiate and impose colonial laws. He can convoke or prorogue the insular legislative body and can dissolve separately or simultaneously either of its branches.

The provision that if this shall be done the legislature must be convoked within three months does not remedy the evil, because its convocation. if it were composed of members opposed to his policy, would be immediately followed by its prorogation. If measures are presented for discussion in the local legislature, the governor-general has the authority to prevent further discussion whenever he may consider that national interests are in any manner affected or in any wise prejudiced thereby.

The result of this power can easily be understood. If a legisla-

ture is selected not subservient to Spanish interests, and measures
are offered legitimate and proper, and discussion ensues displeas-
ing to some tyrannous governor-general, he may say that it affects
national interests, or that any criticism of Spain's policy is inimi-
cal to national prerogatives, and thereupon either prevent further
discussion and refer the question to the Spanish Government for
determination, or dissolve or adjourn the assembly.

If the former course is pursued, the Spanish Government may
hold the matter under advisement for an indefinite period, thereby
effectually preventing legislation and so gagging and stifling the
Cuban representatives that not only would freedom of. speech
be denied, but the assembly itself become a mere pretense and
mockery: Does any member suppose under this system that if
peace should now come it would be of long duration?

It must be evident to every person that disturbed conditions
would manifest themselves immediately and that with the arbi-
trary power possessed by the Governor-General the local assembly
would be adjourned; its representatives would appeal to the people, the latter would vindicate their course, and resort would be
had to arms, and the power and authority of Spain again be challenged. This autonomy is a veritable Pandora's box. It is sur-
charged with bristling problems and difficulties and filled with
so much subtlety and uncertainty, as well as unconcealed fraud
and deceit, that its permanent establishment is an impossibility.

Again, it commits to the Spanish Crown the appointment of the
judiciary. Possibly some of the subordinate tribunals may be
organized and filled by the Cubans, but the higher judicial tribunals and appellate courts are created and controlled by Spain.
A governor of one of the provinces, a Cuban of eminence and integrity, who had been induced to support the autonomist scheme,
stated to me that he insisted that the judges must be selected by
the people themselves; that if this were denied, he would fight autonomy, because its acceptance would not mean a settlement of
the questions at issue.

I called his attention to the fact that but a few days before the
telegraphic dispatches announced the appointment of twelve judges
by the Spanish Government for Cuba and that that very day further dispatches showed the appointment by the Queen Regent of a
member of the appellate court for the island. With Spanish
judges to construe the law there could be no peace. With the
power reserved to Spain to adjudicate through her tribunals every
litigated controversy, not only those affecting property, but those
affecting personal liberty, the most optimistic can not hope for
peace and the settlement of the Cuban question.

Again, article 36 provides:

To the Spanish Cortes belongs the determination of what shall be considered by their nature necessary expenses of the sovereignty, and the Spanish
Cortes will determine every three years its amount and the necessary assets
to cover it, always reserving to itself the right to alter this provision.

This, contrary to the view announced by President McKinley
in his message, is a limitation upon the Cuban parliament and
prevents them from framing "the budget as to expenditures and
revenues," thus committing to the Spanish Government the
power to apportion the expenses of war, of the army and navy, of
diplomatic agents, and the meeting of all liabilities connected
with the sovereignty of the Government.

Who can doubt but what, if peace were now established, with
Cuba as a colonial dependency, the Spanish Government would

at once strengthen her navy, increase her army, and exert every effort to place herself upon a war footing? She would claim, unquestionably, that Cuba would be the beneficiary of this course, and would insist, therefore, that a large portion, perhaps one-third or one-half, of the expenses should be borne by the island. This position would of course be unacceptable to the insulars. Spain would thereupon, by force if necessary, collect from Cuba the amount assigned, and the smoldering fires would at once burst forth, to be quenched only by the blood of another revolution.

There is no adjustment of the public debt. No division is made. and no suggestion as to the proportion which will be exacted of Cuba. This question is postponed until "the termination of the war will allow its final total to be determined." Who determines it? The Spanish Cortes. Who apportions it? The Spanish Government. With the colossal debt of Spain, amounting to more than $1,000,000,000, who can doubt but what Spain will insist that Cuba shall bear a heavy portion of this sum?

With the island impoverished, with property valueless, the sum of two or three hundred million dollars—a greater amount, unquestionably, Spain would insist should be paid by Cuba—would be such a burden that the island could not survive under it. This, then, would provoke complications. A refusal to pay or a default in the payment of the principal or interest would be employed by Spain for enacting further repressive measures and exercising absolute control over the fiscal and other affairs of the island. If the Cubans accept autonomy, they know this weapon of confiscation is in the hands of Spain. The latter's impoverished condition will be too strong a temptation to restrain heavy reprisals upon Cuba. Autonomy permits the Cuban people to control merely their roads and public improvements and matters relating to public health.

In every vital question, in all those matters affecting person and property and liberty and freedom of thought and speech, in those individual, national, and sovereign powers, Spain's hand rests as heavily upon Cuba as ever before. We may search no further than the paper granting autonomy for the reasons leading the Cuban people to its rejection.

The upper branch, or council of administration of the insular cortes, will be controlled by the Crown. Seventeen of its members are appointed directly by the governor-general acting for the sovereign; and the influences of Spain will be so potent, especially when it is remembered that eligibility rests upon an annual income of at least $4,000, that under all circumstances a portion of the remaining eighteen will be the creatures of the parent government.

Granting that this royal decree is bona fide and is designed as a measure of administrative reform, it has not been vitalized by approval of the Cortes. It is inchoate. incomplete, merely a temporary proclamation which may be withdrawn at the pleasure of the ministry or nullified by the Spanish Cortes. To this criticism of the autonomistic decree Dr. Congosto and members of the cabinet stated to me that Spain's honor was involved in its sacred maintenance. and that inasmuch as it was the result of "evolution," and that reforms once promulgated can never be repealed, the Cubans were under obligation to accept. depending upon the honor of the Spanish people to impress it with the seal of organic law and honestly execute its provisions.

This answer is unsatisfactory to the Cubans. They say that

Spain's unfulfilled promises of reform, made at the treaty of Zanjon, caused the existing war. They also say that it is significant that no step has been taken to submit Sagasta's "wooden horse" plan to the Cortes for approval. How can Spain, that knows nothing of freedom, that lives in the mediævalism of the past, governed by a bureaucratic system, with a shadowy legislative body to validate, when called upon, the decrees of nobles selected by the Crown, design a system of honest, liberal, true colonial government?

How can she give that which she does not possess and has no conception of? Yet this is the offering which the President says will give local government to Cuba; and this deceptive decree has prevented this Government from courageously dealing with a question which, each day undisposed of, becomes more complicated. This nation's high mission is not to aid in the enslavement of a people; yet our present policy is a glorification of "autonomy" and a support of Spain's effort in chaining it upon the necks of the Cuban people.

Among the hundreds of people with whom I spoke, including the rich and the poor, the Spaniard and the volunteer, the Cuban planter, the reconcentrado, the starving peasant, the insurgent in arms, I found less than a dozen persons who sincerely and earnestly believed in autonomy and zealously labored for its implantation. The Spaniards (most of whom belong to the conservative party) bitterly assailed it.

When asked for the grounds of their opposition, they failed to disclose any, although it was apparent their opposition was largely the result of the failure of General Blanco to consult them or select from their numbers the various persons who were being intrusted with office. The policy of Weyler they heartily indorsed. The atrocities and crimes committed during his régime seemed rather to meet their approval; and this is paradoxical, because many of them in their private life are compassionate and humane, and in their business affairs are industrious, honest, frugal, and materially aid in the advancement and development of the island.

At this point, a matter suggests itself, which a student of sociology would regard with interest. Nearly all the Spaniards in Cuba are males. They came to Cuba in their youth, hoping by industry and frugality to amass a competency, and return in the afternoon of life to enjoy its calm and quiet in the beautiful land of their nativity. They faithfully devote themselves to labor, and soon become merchants or traders or interested in some business venture. They form the shoppers and traders and brokers of the island.

Though their patrons are Cubans and their wealth is made from Cubans, and though they owe their all to Cuba and her fertility, they are the implacable enemies of the Cuban people. Most of those who marry select their wives from Cuban families, but their hostility to all other Cubans still continues. Their children, carefully guarded by the mothers, grow up as Cubans. They love their fathers, but are imbued with strong prejudices against all other Spaniards.

While the father is thinking only of his business and dreaming only of the day when he may return to the scenes of his childhood, his son thinks only of Cuba and longs for the day when, as an independent nation, her flag shall float on land and sea. So in the Spanish family there are the seeds of discord and revolution. When Marti, Gomez, and Maceo raised the standard of revolt, the

3223—2

sons of Spaniards were the first to support it, and during all the dark hours of this struggle they have never faltered, and many have willingly and joyfully given their lives for the cause of Cuban independence.

A prominent Spanish merchant, whose son was with General Garcia, sorrowfully, but with some anger, in speaking of the Spaniards residing in Cuba, said to me:

We are at fault for the revolution. We have been so occupied in our business that we have let our wives rear our children and teach them treason.

I found no just reason for the professed optimism of General Blanco, Congosto, Montero, and the supporters of the autonomistic régime. The Marquis Montero assured me that in every town I would find well-organized clubs of autonomists, composed of Cubans and Spaniards, and men who had formerly been "separatists"—that is, those who desired independence—and the most pronounced "intransigentes"—that is, the most loyal Spaniards—and that with the support of these organizations the administration was confident the people would soon accept autonomy.

I was further told by Dr. Congosto, and my investigations verified the truth of the statement, that every alcalde and governor in the island belonged to the autonomist party. But the conversations which I had with leading autonomists convinced me that, with but few exceptions, they had no faith in the plan and would give a doubtful allegiance to it. To popularize the system, Blanco had taken persons who had been imprisoned by Weyler and placed them in responsible positions.

The offices were being filled by Cubans, not Spaniards. The reasons for this were manifest when Señor Galvez (president of the new ministry) said, that "when this plan is put into operation, if the war continues, it will be Cubans fighting Cubans, and no longer a contest between Cubans and Spaniards." The evident design of Blanco is to win prominent Cubans to this delusive phantom by giving them high positions, hoping thereby to secure the support of the Cuban people. That inglorious, humiliating defeat will attend this effort must be patent even to the proponents of the measure.

Without discussing the ethical question involved in such conduct, I state it to be a fact that many of those holding official positions heartily sympathize with the insurgents and earnestly desire the independence of Cuba. Some frankly confess that they accepted the positions, fearful that if they refused, imprisonment would follow. Others stated that their acceptance resulted merely from a desire to alleviate, if possible, the horrors and sufferings of their fellow-countrymen, the reconcentrados. One high official aided me in passing the Spanish lines to confer with the insurgent forces, and another with fervid enthusiasm informed me of the purposes and plans of the insurgents and the triumphant victory which would soon be theirs.

I visited autonomist clubs, and found the members not only openly expressing sympathy for the revolution, but secretly contributing to its success. I talked with the poor reconcentrados, and asked if they did not think it wise for all to renew their allegiance to Spain. Many had suffered so terribly and were so ravenous for food that questions of governmental polity were as uninviting as a proposition in calculus. But the hearts and hopes of all were with their fathers and brothers and husbands and countrymen in the tragic struggle which brought such unutterable woes, such desolation and death.

3223

The few Cubans who could obtain employment, whether they were whites or blacks, were robbing themselves and their families in order to contribute of their mite to their comrades in arms. I met a gentleman, once wealthy, now wanting for food for himself and family, who gave the insurgents his last cow the day of my visit to him. The women and children, the Cuban lawyer, the native doctor, the workman, the humblest farmer, the poorest peasant, and the negro in the field, all are Cubans and all are revolutionists. Wherever is found a Cuban home, there stands an altar dedicated to Cuba libre, and each home is a fortress protecting freedom's cause, while within all earnestly, prayerfully watch for the coming of the day of liberation.

All efforts to win the insurgents to the autonomist plan have proven abortive. I met emissaries sent by Blanco to various provinces, and they confessed that their missions had been fruitless. One of them, Mr. Laces, who had been in the Orient for the purpose of seeing the president and vice-president of the Cuban Republic, stated to me that—

The Cuban forces in the eastern provinces are intensely hostile to autonomy. They are determined upon independence. It will be a long time before we can hope to win them to our cause.

I talked with insurgents, and they declared they would never abandon their struggle until the Spanish armies were driven from the island and the independence of Cuba established. Blanco is resorting to every possible means to win the insurgent leaders to his support. Offices, prominent positions, and great inducements, including monetary bribes and considerations, are held out to them; but thus far the insurgents have been unmoved.

A few who have been wounded or are suffering from serious illness have become "presentados," but when health returns they rejoin their companies. A few malcontents have surrendered to the Spanish armies. Governor Garcia, of the province of Santa Clara, stated to me that a prominent Cuban officer would surrender, or "present" himself, upon the following day, together with 100 of his followers.

The invitation was extended me to accompany the governor upon a special train and witness the "presentation." I accepted, but when the next day arrived, no insurgents appeared. The governor promised to telegraph me as soon as the officer surrendered, but to this hour no telegram has been received.

I met a doctor who had charge of the insurgent hospitals in two provinces. He traveled constantly among the troops, having visited several thousand within the few days immediately preceding my interview with him. He stated that there was no disposition upon the part of either the officers or soldiers to accept autonomy; that it was treated with derision and scorn, and regarded as a subtle device to induce the Cuban patriots to lay down their arms.

An officer in the insurgent ranks told me that if genuine autonomy had been offered before Weyler's cruelties and atrocities had been perpetrated, he thought the Cubans would have accepted it; but that now, after hundreds of thousands of their countrymen had been butchered and starved, and the island had been desolated by fire and sword, and the homes of the insurgents had been destroyed and their wives and children either brutally killed by Spanish troops or imprisoned until, by hunger and privation, death had been a welcome release, they would never abandon the conflict until Spain's sovereignty was extinct and the Republic of

Cuba firmly established. I met one insurgent soldier who had secretly entered a village in order to learn of his family. His wife and six children had been buried in the trench. Weyler had killed them. Starvation was his weapon. Could he accept autonomy?

The volunteers, of whom so much has been heard, number from 25,000 to 40,000. Resident Spaniards of Cuba compose the volunteer corps. They are the most uncompromising foes of Cubans, the friends of Weyler, the opponents of autonomy. They are the controlling factor in Habana. They believe in the prosecution of the war, even to the extent of exterminating the Cubans.

With the Spanish soldiers and the Spanish residents against autonomy, with the insurgents in the field fighting for independence and rejecting the proffers of peace predicated upon an acceptance of autonomy, with all of the Cuban noncombatants secretly opposing it and clandestinely supporting the insurgents, it must be apparent that autonomy is already defeated and that any further delay upon the part of this Government in dealing definitely with the Cuban question, based upon the idea that autonomy will prove the solution of the question, will be the height of fatuity and a tribute to our credulity and ignorance.

In this connection reference should be made to the condition of the troops and the prospect of Spanish victories. When the revolution began, February 14, 1895, there were 20,320 Spanish soldiers and 60,000 volunteers in Cuba. In March 7,000 additional soldiers arrived. Weyler asked for 200,000, and at least 125,000 were sent in response to his call. To-day less than 60,000 Spanish troops are in the island. Disease, superinduced by privation and hunger, destroyed most of the Spanish troops. The hospitals contain 15,000, and from 1,200 to 1,800 are returned to Spain each month.

The Spanish soldiers now upon the island are young boys, poorly fed and imperfectly clothed. Many of them stated to me, though, that their condition was very much improved since the advent of General Blanco. From all that I could learn, General Weyler treated his troops in a most inhuman manner. He suffered his officers and contractors to rob them of their small stipend and deprive them of the necessary food and clothing. They were stationed in small forts and left to die of starvation and fever.

Notwithstanding all these sufferings and privations, and though the Government is in arrears in its payment of the troops, from eight to twelve months, I found the soldiers uncomplaining, faithful, apparently unconcerned as to the progress of the war or the disposition to be made of them. I believe they are brave and courageous and obedient in executing any order given them.

Of the Spanish officers but little commendable can be said. They are indolent, idle, selfish, unpatriotic, absolutely indifferent to the situation and the perils of the country which they serve. They are found in the cafés, promenades, theaters, and everywhere but in the barracks or in the field or engaged in active service. More officers than soldiers are to be seen in the cities. I counted nearly 150 in a small theater in Habana during an operatic performance.

An intelligent campaign with the resources and soldiers at Weyler's command must necessarily have resulted in the subjugation of the revolutionists. But Spain's opportunity has passed. There have been no campaigns, no military operations, upon the part of the Spaniards worthy the name. I saw no drilling and found but few persons who had ever seen the Spanish troops drill.

The soldiers sent from Spain are, in the main, raw recruits, boys without military training, from the mountains and valleys and farms and shops. Immediately upon their arrival they are sent into the interior, placed in small forts, many of which are located in swamps and lowlands, and there left to the ravages of hunger and fevers. At present most of the Spanish troops are employed in protecting towns and cities and guarding a few plantations and the railroad trains and tracks.

General Pando is operating in the "Orient," but is utterly unable to dislodge the insurgents. The armies under Gomez are stronger to-day, better equipped and disciplined than ever before. I learned this not only from conversations with insurgents, but from statements made by Spanish officers and officials. One of the commissioners sent by Blanco into the Oriente told me that in the provinces of Puerto Principe and Santiago de Cuba there were at least 35,000 well armed and equipped insurgents.

In the Province of Santa Clara the insurgent forces number 2,000; in Matanzas, 1,800; in Habana, 1,500, and in Pinar del Rio, 2,500. A letter which I hold in my hand, from General Rodriguez, the insurgent commander of the three provinces last named, states that the condition of the troops was never better; that in health and spirits they are superb, and that they have all the arms required, but are somewhat deficient in clothing.

If Spain was unable, with the magnificent army under Weyler's generalship, to reconquer Cuba, it is difficult to understand how success upon the battlefields can now crown her efforts. With $12,000,000 required each month for the army, with her treasury exhausted, and her forces so limited that only police duty is done, the contest can only end in Cuban success. One of the Spanish officials, with rather an air of pride, called my attention to a dispatch stating that Spain was negotiating for a loan of 200,000,000 pesetas, offering as security a second mortgage upon custom-house receipts to be collected in Cuba and the cédula tax thereafter to be levied and collected in the island.

When it is remembered that already mortgages have been given upon the prospective revenues of the island for years, and also that the cédula tax is based upon the income of the insulars, it is evident the security offered would not be accepted by any money lender.

When I asked General Uberto, who commanded the Spanish troops in Santa Clara Province, how he expected Spanish success when the insurgents were now stronger than ever and the Spanish armies weaker, his reply was evasive, being an appeal to the chivalry and pride of Spain, which, "under every danger, would never submit to defeat." He bitterly complained of the United States, charging that the revolution was attributable to this Government and its continued violation of treaty obligations as well as omission to prevent fillibustering expeditions.

When attention was called to the fact that Spain's ships and vessels had intercepted no craft, but that so rigorously had police duty been performed by this Government that numerous expeditions had been prevented and vessels captured, he was compelled to confess that no breach of duty could be charged against the United States. He then complained that our sympathies for the insurgents inspired them to resistance, and that the United States was the real enemy of Spain, masquerading behind the armies of Gomez.

C223

This spirit of animosity I found to be prevalent with the Spanish officers and many of the Spanish residents. No military expeditions were being conducted and no campaigns carried on by the Spanish generals. They contented themselves with guarding the cities and towns, and attempting to protect a few plantations and the railroad trains and tracks. There were no tents or vehicles, and no commissary department connected with the army. The idea of leaving the towns and railroads and pursuing the insurgents into the interior seemed not to be a part of the programme.

In the four provinces last named the Spanish troops hold by a more or less precarious tenure the cities, towns, and railroads, but the rest of the country is occupied by the insurgents. The latter go at pleasure, occasionally approaching the little blockhouses, frequently intercepting trains and destroying bridges, and often breaking through the fortifications, in the darkness of night, and plundering some store or warehouse in the smaller villages.

Upon each train soldiers are placed to protect it, and armored cars filled with soldiers precede it. Each railroad station is a fortress, and upon each side of the railroad track, every few hundred yards, is a small fort or blockhouse filled with Spanish soldiers to protect the track. A few plantations are operated, but these are protected by forts constructed at the expense of the owners and garrisoned by Spanish soldiers, for each of which $30 per month is paid to the Spanish commanders.

Beyond the range of the forts, as stated, the country is in the hands of the insurgents. Within the range of the forts there is some agricultural activity. I met insurgents within a few miles of Spanish forts and within 2 miles of important cities. The day after reaching Habana Aranguren and his forces approached within a few miles of the city and destroyed a costly bridge. The camp of one of the insurgent leaders was within 18 miles of Habana, and when I was in the city of Matanzas General Betencourt was hovering upon its outskirts.

In each of the so-called pacified provinces, civil officers of the Cuban Republic are engaged in superintending extensive fields, within which are raised sweet potatoes and various fruits and vegetables for the sustenance of the insurgent armies. The Spaniards, the Cuban noncombatants, and the Spanish troops are locked up in the cities and fortifications, while the insurgents, with but slight resistance, freely roam over these four provinces.

This is the extent of the pacification. An insurgent captain informed me that the policy of Gomez was to "wear Spain out; to compel the troops to garrison the cities and towns, thus preventing their mobilization and any attempt to enter upon an aggressive military campaign." Occasionally a Spanish general with a few thousand troops will make a hurried dash into the country and a brief encounter with the Cubans may result.

In the two eastern provinces some spirited engagements are occurring. The efforts of Pando to penetrate the interior have been repulsed and he has been compelled to return to Habana. It is evident that under this state of warfare, if Spain is able to maintain her troops in the island, the contest may be prolonged indefinitely. It has been charged that the insurgents are barbarous negroes, and that the contest has degenerated into a mere guerrilla warfare.

There is some little foundation for the latter criticism. But it is impossible to prescribe any definite rules for conducting war.

The plan of Gomez has certainly been successful in weakening his adversaries, in destroying the Spanish armies, and in wresting provinces from Spanish control; and this has been done, too, in the main, with due regard to the rights of Spanish prisoners.

That the insurgents do not risk their cause upon a single battle, is true; that they avoid meeting a well-armed superior force, must also be conceded; but that their policy depletes the ranks of the enemy and exhausts the treasury of Spain, and daily weakens the military strength of their enemy, all must admit. If the results are the same as might be achieved by two or three victorious battles, who shall say that it is not war? But, as stated, occasionally there are fierce engagements between large contending forces.

The Cuban armies are composed of about 80 per cent negroes and mulattoes; the remainder are white Cubans. The negroes are brave, courageous, intelligent, and patriotic. When the war began, thousands of the brightest young white Cubans in the island, flocked to the standard of Gomez, and hundreds who were being educated in the colleges of France and the United States hastened to give their support to the revolution.

Within its ranks are found thousands of brave, heroic men of education and refinement, men who have in our schools and colleges, imbibed the spirit of liberty and the love of republican institutions. There are so many professional men in the Cuban army that it is sometimes called the "doctors' and lawyers' war." The insurgents are not wild bandits or guerrillas, but are men worthy of the blessings of freedom, capable of appreciating liberty, and with capacity to maintain a stable, enlightened, liberal government. By appointment I met one of these young leaders. He had been educated in the United States and Paris.

The revolution found him the possessor of the luxuries and comforts of wealth, and yet he gladly left all to cast his fortunes with those who entered upon the struggle for Cuban independence. For nearly three years he had been wandering through the provinces, hunted and pursued by the Spanish troops, suffering exposure and disease, but he is still inflexible in his purpose and happy in his undertaking. He assured me that there would be no compromise, no surrender, but that the revolution would continue until Cuba was free.

In the four western provinces the insurgents operate in small companies, but there is such discipline and system that mobilization can be effected very quickly. An organization which permits an army to almost disintegrate, and yet has such control as to mass the troops and concentrate its full strength within a few days, is not only marvelous, but indicates a high order of generalship, upon the part of the military leaders as well as great devotion upon the part of both officers and men. To keep Spain's forces dispersed is a strong reason for this mode of warfare. In addition, the impoverished condition of the island and the difficulty in securing food render it hazardous to move in large bodies.

The two eastern provinces comprise about one-half the area of the island. These provinces, with the exception of a few cities, are absolutely dominated by the insurgents. Spain's authority has been completely overthrown, and the Cuban Republic is exercising, with but little molestation or opposition, undisputed control. The civil officers perform their functions, and the civil machinery is in constant operation. President Masso and his cabinet remain at the capital—Cubitas—during most of the time and perform the constitutional duties enjoined upon them.

Weyler, with nearly 200,000 troops and volunteers, found it impossible to successfully invade these provinces. His troops were hurled back like the waves of the ocean, whenever any advance was made. In the four western provinces, in which the Spanish claim the fruits of their success are apparent and the evidences of peace and pacification appear, there is nothing but desolation, ruin, starvation, and death. In the hundreds of miles that I traveled there was no sign of life outside of the forts and the fortified cities, towns, and plantations.

The island for 400 miles in length is a wilderness. The fertility of the island, however, is so great that though flame and sword may desolate it, the grass and verdure soon cover it and render less hideous the work of destruction. Every farm in these four provinces has been destroyed, every house except in the cities and towns and upon a few fortified plantations has been burned, all farm implements and property of a personal character have either been carried away or fed to the flames which swept over the island. The horses and cattle have been driven from the fields and long since confiscated either by the Spanish troops or the insurgent forces.

That General Blanco has made some reform and abated somewhat the severities of Weyler's administration can not be doubted; yet he rigorously enforces the rule which prevents the people who are herded in the fortified cities and towns from going beyond the lines of the fortifications and attempting the rebuilding of their homes or the effort to procure from the soil enough for their subsistence.

Weyler's order of reconcentration drove into the cities and towns at least 600,000 people. Their homes and property were destroyed and many of the people ruthlessly butchered. The Spanish troops and guerrillas, without, in many instances, giving them any opportunity to understand the order or make any preparation, enforced their departure from their homes and brutally drove them like cattle into the adjacent cities and towns. Around the latter, deep trenches had been constructed and upon the ramparts thrown up, posts and palisades were planted and bound and strengthened by barbed wire.

These suffering, wretched people found themselves in these cities without clothing or food or roof or shelter. Any attempt to cross the trocha to return to their blackened homes or to search in the desolate fields for roots or sweet potatoes for themselves or their suffering, starving wives and children, subjected them to being shot by the soldiers guarding; or if they were successful in escaping their vigilant eye, they encountered the Spanish guerrillas, by whom they were cruelly dispatched and brought into the city, thrown into the streets as a warning to others, and their death made the foundation for a dispatch of a Spanish victory over insurgent forces. Thus imprisoned, they became first desperate, then sullen, and at last, in pathetic despair, sat down in the streets and highways listlessly awaiting the approach of death.

Those who have property, behold it gradually wasting, and those who have none are daily meeting death from exposure and starvation. I met hundreds of people who had been wealthy, but whose property was valueless. American citizens who owned hundreds and thousands of acres were homeless and offering extensive tracts of lands for a small pittance with which to purchase bread.

Within the range of the rifle's ball, around the cities and towns and upon the few fortified plantations, a few persons are at work in the fields. To leave the cities or pass beyond the line of forts is impossible without a passport, unless under cover of the darkness of the night. The surviving reconcentrados are prevented from returning to their desolate lands, and even if permission were accorded them, the difficulties before them are great. Emaciated by long privations, without homes or utensils or implements of any kind, without horses or cattle, their return would be like a visit to a wilderness, and their subsistence dependent upon its subjugation.

Inadequate efforts are being made for their support. General Blanco stated that he had been authorized to use $100,000 to feed the reconcentrados; but this amount, when nearly 200.000 people are wanting food and clothes, and many of them medicines and shelter, would but slightly mitigate their sufferings.

And so, while they are confined by Spanish forts and rifles, and prevented from tilling the soil or seeking subsistence, the charitable of this nation are being called upon to contribute to relieve their extremities. While Spain is attempting to exterminate them by this hopeless war, we are only prolonging their sufferings by the meager contributions expended in their behalf.

From personal investigations and figures furnished me by Spaniards, governors of provinces, mayors of cities, priests, doctors, and various officials, it is my firm conviction that not less than 300,000 people have died from starvation and diseases superinduced by these privations during the year 1897 in the four provinces in which the order of reconcentration was enforced. And if the war shall be prolonged, or this Government shall not intervene either for the preservation of the people or to restore peace and secure the independence of the island, more than 100,000 people will meet death from starvation within the next few months.

In the city of Habana from 25,000 to 30,000 people are in absolute want. Many are dying daily from starvation and the deprivations they have endured. Thousands haunt your footsteps in the streets, their only resting place being the cold pavements. In Guines more than one-half of the population, made up of the residents and those driven in by Weyler's troops, died during the year of 1897. In Artimesa, in the Province of Pinar del Rio, from 40 to 60 per cent of the population perished from the same causes during the same period.

The governor of Matanzas Province stated to me that official reports showed that nearly 40,000 persons in the reconcentrado towns and cities within that province had died from May, 1897, to the 31st of December of the same year. Investigation proved that these reports did not cover those who had not been buried under the auspices of the church. One of the alcaldes in the same province and several reputable physicians, as well as a very prominent Spaniard who had been an alcalde, stated that the deaths were very much in excess of the figure furnished by the governor.

Governor Armas seemed a very humane man and claimed to be doing what he could to alleviate the sufferings; but it was apparent that very little was being accomplished in that direction. Upon the steps of his palace, as I was returning to the hotel late in the evening, I saw fourteen starving, half-naked creatures lying upon the stone steps. The next morning I learned that several had died during the night.

In the streets of the city of Matanzas, in which he resided, the scenes of distress and suffering were almost unendurable. Starv-

8223

ing mothers with their starving children were encountered at every corner. I saw several men who had once been strong lying dead in the streets. In improvised hospitals in the suburbs of the city were hundreds of these unfortunate reconcentrados. The young boy in control of one informed me that 1 in 20 who entered the hospital passed out alive.

I accompanied him while administering the food furnished for the day. It consisted of 4 quarts of milk and about 25 pounds of rice for about 300 persons. Many were so emaciated and had suffered so long for the lack of food that they were unable to take the few spoonsful offered them. None were suffering from disease, except such as resulted from starvation. In passing the next morning I learned that thirteen had died during the night. In other places visited the same distressing, horrible sights were presented.

In Colon, Jucaro, Cruzes, Manzanillo, Santa Clara, Sagua la Grande, San Domingo, Guanabacoa, and indeed in every town and city visited, these awful, harrowing scenes could not be escaped. From all that I could learn no efforts whatever had been made during Weyler's administration for the relief of the people. Indeed, I met persons who had been in the Cabanas fortress for furnishing medicines and food to the dying and starving. I met noble, heroic women who had been thrust into dungeons for attempting to supply quinine to the dying reconcentrados.

Even now there is lack of organization, and what little is being accomplished for the people results from the efforts of the Cubans, with occasional help from some humane Spaniard. It seems as though the people are so inured to the sufferings that they have grown somewhat apathetic. The alcalde of Sagua la Grande stated that 10,000 in that city needed immediate help. He had organized committees and was doing everything within his power to ameliorate the fearful condition. He had gathered sufficient means to furnish for five or six days a few ounces of beans and rice to 1,600 of the most distressed.

This deplorable condition, so briefly and imperfectly sketched, demonstrates that the reason assigned by the President for inaction does not exist, and that Sagasta has not wrought such changes or reforms as to restrain this Government from altering its "do-nothing" policy.

Our doubtful, hesitating course has added to our embarrassments. And it is clear that stronger reasons exist for granting belligerency to the Cubans than were found two years ago. I shall contend, before concluding my remarks, that immediate intervention by the United States is not only now justifiable but imperatively required. Before proceeding with a discussion of this question I desire to consider the first point made by President McKinley, to which I called attention a few minutes ago, namely, that under the principles of international law the Cuban insurgents were not entitled to belligerent rights.

The President quotes at length from the message of President Grant delivered to Congress December 7, 1875, in which the latter argued that unless justified by necessity the granting of belligerency had always been, and justly, regarded as an unfriendly act and a gratuitous demonstration of moral support to the rebellion; and further, that there was no such "substantial political organization, real, palpable, and manifest to the world, among the Cubans as to take the contest out of the category of a mere rebellious insurrection and place it on the footing of war."

3223

President McKinley approves of the views expressed by General Grant, and contends that the possession of the essential qualifications of sovereignty and the adoption in the conduct of the war of rules approved by the received code of war are lacking in the Cuban revolution, and that "without the attributes of statehood," the existence of which he considers doubtful, the recognition of belligerency would be "inadmissible and indefensible."

I have shown that in 1896 the present Secretary of State and the gentleman from Illinois [Mr. HITT], as well as other distinguished Republicans, not only contended that the revolution in Cuba, measured by the rules of international law, had reached such position that it was justly entitled to belligerent rights, but that with great unanimity the Republicans in both branches of Congress voted for such a resolution.

I have also shown that time has only added strength to the revolution and subtracted from the power of the titular government. Belligerency is merely a state of war, and war "is that state in which a nation prosecutes its right by force." Whether war exists is a question of fact, and that fact is to be determined by each neutral nation for itself.

In a letter from Canovas to the New York World, March 6, 1896, Spain's great minister admits that the struggle is a "civil war," and declares " it is impossible to attempt reforms during a civil war or under any foreign pressure in the present condition of the island." Minister De Lome, in a letter to Clara Barton, dated February 12, 1897, unwittingly confessed that the insurrection in Cuba reached the dignity of public war. As early as January 7, 1896, La Pais, a leading Spanish newspaper, contained these words:

We hold in front of our troops 53,000 insurgents. Thirty thousand of them are well mounted and perfectly armed.

It seems absurd for the President and gentlemen upon the other side of the Chamber to argue that a condition of public war does not exist in Cuba. Neither a de jure nor a de facto government is indispensable to belligerency. It is not imperative that the revolutionary forces should occupy seaports or whiten the ocean with their sails. Yet this is the contention in the President's message and of our Republican friends.

It is not the location of the civil government, nor its capacity to command the allegiance, the support, or the obedience of the people outside of the domain of its military command, but inside that territory, that fixes its right to recognition as a belligerent power. A de facto civil government having power to enforce obedience to its decrees within its military command, whether that power is civil or military, is a government that can conduct lawful warfare under the laws of nations. It needs no capital, or seaports, or garrisoned fortresses to prove its right to fight for the liberties of its supporters.

The present premier of Spain, Señor Sagasta, in his speech before a meeting of the Liberal senators and deputies on the 19th of May, 1897, substantially admits that the insurgents were a belligerent power, and if not a de facto government, were sufficiently organized to enforce obedience to decrees within its military command. These are his words:

We have 200,000 troops in Cuba, but we are not even masters of the territory trodden by our soldiers. The picture could not be gloomier. We have war in Cuba and in the Philippines.

3223

Toussaint had no treasury or navy or harbor. France possessed each; yet Toussaint and his supporters were belligerents, and San Domingo became an independent republic.

In our own revolutionary struggles we had a floating capital, our Treasury was empty, and our harbors were possessed by England; yet under every rule of international law our fathers were belligerents.

It must not be forgotten that many of the principles of international law are an unwelcome legacy from the past. They were evolved by despotic governments in the interests of power and to preserve kingly prerogatives. The rights of man, the questions of liberty and free government, the duties which a high civilization and a true Christianity impose, were of less concern than kingly power and the perpetuity of oppressive government.

Our nation has made great contributions to international law, and the growth of personal liberty has found reflex action in international codes. International law is not an exact science and must expand to meet the currents that rush on to wider and nobler spheres. The view of the President, as well as that of General Grant, seems to be founded upon the position taken by Mr. Dana in his notes to Wheaton's International Law.

The question of "necessity" is not involved, in according belligerent rights. Where any considerable part of a nation seeks withdrawal therefrom and in good faith takes up arms and combats the titular government for the purpose of obtaining political ends; when, as the Cubans have done, it maintains the conflict for years and supports a military organization capable of executing such degrees as are essential not only for its organization but for the effective discomfiture of its opponent, and where there is a civil power operating within constitutional limits, feeble though its authority may be, the movement assumes such proportions as to remove its supporters from the category of criminals, and stamps as barbarous their treatment as pirates. Therefore they are belligerents, and nations friendly to the parent government should so regard them and maintain a strict neutrality between the contending powers. And it is the exclusive province of the neutral government to determine when the revolution ceases to be a piratical expedition or a criminal insurrection, and its promoters entitled to neutrality. I desire to present some authorities in support of the views just announced.

Judge Grier, in the prize cases (2 Black), says:

A civil war is never solemnly declared. It becomes such by accident. The power and organizations of the persons who originate and carry it on, when the party in rebellion occupy and hold in a hostile manner a certain portion of territory, have declared their independence and cast off their allegiance, have organized armies, commenced hostilities against their former sovereign, the world acknowledges them as belligerents and the contest as war.

Mr. Manning, in his valuable work (page 98), announces this to be the rule:

The concession of such rights may at a certain epoch of the strife be claimed both in the interests of humanity and of neutral states; there always, indeed, arrives a moment at which such a concession is made (as in the case of the late Southern insurrection in the United States) by the government from which the revolt takes place.

Speaking of the time when the recognition of belligerency may be accorded, he says:

It must be neither so premature as to embarrass a friendly government in suppressing what may prove to be only a transient or partial display of disorder or treachery, nor, on the other hand, so dilatory as to protract the inconvenience and cruelty incident to a contest conducted on a large scale, apart from all the humane alleviations which the laws of civilized war have introduced.

Earl Russell, replying to Mr. Seward's criticisms of England in recognizing the belligerency of the Confederacy, referred in justification to the number of troops employed by the United States and its vast preparations for war. It is now conceded by all that England's action was conformable to the law of nations, especially in view of the fact that President Lincoln by his proclamation relating to the blockade treated the Confederates as belligerents.

Vattel (page 299) declares that—

> When a party is formed in a state who no longer obeys the sovereign, and are possessed of sufficient strength to oppose him, this is called civil war.

And Hall, in his great work on international law, announces the principle that clearly brings the Cubans within its terms. He states:

> As soon as a considerable population is arrayed in arms with the professed object of obtaining political ends, it resembles a state too nearly for it to be possible to treat individuals belonging to such population as criminals. It would be inhuman for the enemy to execute its prisoners. It would be still more inhuman for foreign nations to capture and hang the crews of the war ships as pirates. Humanity requires that the members of such a community be treated as belligerents.

Bluntschli, the German writer, clearly proves that the Cuban insurgents are not mere lawless banditti, conducting, as the President's position implies, a mere criminal resistance against the Government, but are a people engaged in a political revolution, and are therefore entitled to be regarded, not only by Spain, but other nations, as belligerents. The rule is announced by him as follows:

> Every struggle with the armed band, even when it may be organized in a military manner, is not war. When in southern Italy brigands form themselves into armed troops regularly commanded and give battle to the Government troops, they do not for that reason constitute a belligerent party, but only bands of malefactors. The distinction rests upon this: That war is a political struggle, engaged in for political ends. Brigands neither aspire to defend the existing political system nor to create a new one. They only obey the guilty desire by obtaining by violence control of the persons and possessions of their neighbors. They properly fall, therefore, within the jurisdiction of criminal tribunals, and the law of nations is not concerned with them.
>
> It is a different matter when, in a State, a large party of citizens, or subjects, convinced of the necessity of a revolution or the justice of their claim, take up arms, organize themselves in a military manner and oppose regular troops to the troops of the Government. It can not be maintained that such an organized body of citizens, animated by political purpose, does not possess a possible aptitude for the creation of a new state.

It will be seen from this statement that a civil government is not a requisite to a state of belligerency. To contend that Gomez and the heroic men who are following him, that Masso and the civil officials who are subordinate to him are mere brigands, and are to be treated as traitors and malefactors, is shocking to the sensibilities of every person; and yet a refusal to accord them belligerent rights ignores their political aspirations and the tyrannous exactions imposed by Spain, which have led to the revolution and the desire for the creation of a new state, and, by every rule of logic, necessarily requires us to regard them as traitors and pirates.

The Cubans as belligerents, so far as international law is concerned, would have a status merely for the purpose of fighting and (by the arbitrament of the sword) determining whether further

32.3

recognition shall be given them as a distinct and independent nation. The author last mentioned further states:

The quality of belligerency is accorded to armed parties who, without having received from an already existing state the right to combat with armed forces, have militarily organized themselves and struggle in good faith within their own state for a political right.

Professor Snow, late of Harvard University, states the international rule as follows:

A mixed war is a war between members of the same political society. It is a civil war, though it may not reach beyond the proportions of an insurrection or a local rebellion. The movements in Spain in 1866 and 1867 were of this nature. Such a war may attain sufficient strength and magnitude to entitle both contending parties to all the rights of war with respect to each other and to neutral states. Again, according to the manner and degree of the hostile operation, wars are said to be perfect or imperfect.

With the Cuban forces occupying the eastern half of the island and possessing the residue, with the exception of the fortified cities and towns, can it truthfully be said that it is not a civil war?

Dr. Lorimer, in his Institutes of the Law of Nations, announces the rule relative to belligerency as follows:

There is the recognition of the inchoate state as a jural claimant for separate recognition; that is to say, the acknowledgment of its right to contend for its recognition, or, to borrow a phrase from municipal law, of "its title to sue." The form which recognition usually assumes at this stage is that of a concession of belligerent rights.

Professor Pomeroy, in his excellent work on International Law, with great clearness presents the legal principles involved in this subject. He contends that the de facto existence of the insurgents as a state is not an essential prerequisite to the granting of belligerency, and that the government according belligerent rights does not ally itself with the revolutionists, but—

Simply accords to this community the international right to carry on proper war with the usual immunities and duties as to other nations which belong to war. * * * It does not assume to decide upon the justice of the quarrel. * * * Without this recognition all other powers would be under the necessity of treating the insurgents under certain circumstances as outlaws and pirates, for as the community has no standing as a state, it could not without the species of recognition in question perform any hostile act or have recourse to any military measure that might interfere with the rights of other nations, although such acts and measures are permitted to the states by international law.

He contends that to refuse recognition under some circumstances might—

Have the direct effect of causing the states so refusing to take the part of the mother country against the rebels. As a consequence, if another power should remain strictly neutral to the contest, that very attitude must involve the recognition of the insurgents as belligerents. Unless another power desires to take an active part in the hostilities and throw the weight of its influence and, under some circumstances, the positive aid of its executive power in favor of the mother country, it must treat the rebels as belligerents. The propositions, therefore, which I lay down and maintain are, first, that as, in general, every nation has a right to remain neutral in every such contest, every nation has a right to recognize both parties as belligerents, the contest as proper war, and the mother country would have no legal ground of complaint of such act and attitude; secondly, that in general it is the duty of every other nation to take this position of neutrality.

The position of Mr. Dana (which has become the fortress behind which the present Executive protects himself) that there must be a de facto political organization, sufficient in character, population, and resources to constitute, if left to itself, a state among the nations, and the employment of military forces on each side acting in accordance with the rules and customs of war, and the treatment of captured insurgents by the parent state, as prisoners of war, before belligerency can be granted, is not supported by authority. As Professor Pomeroy states:

> The error which lies at the bottom of all Mr. Dana's argument, and which vitiates the whole of it, is the assumption that "necessity" alone would justify the foreign state in recognizing the belligerency of the insurgent community.

The United States in refusing belligerency to the insurgents have been the supporters of Spain, and such refusal is an act of hostility to the Cubans. Civil war exists. This is an incontestable fact. Whether our support of Spain by denying belligerency has been material, actual, and effective may be questioned by some, but that it has been moral, is too palpable to need argument. Spain had no right to require this "moral" aid from us. The insurgents would be justified in complaining because of its bestowal. Spain demands the right to determine whether the contest is war. The same right of determination belongs to this Government. Our action in granting belligerency might not influence Spain. She might still regard the insurgents as pirates and treat them as such. But no law, national or international, ought to require this nation to treat them as criminals. In the controversy we should have been neutral. If neutrality had been observed, belligerency would have been accorded the supporters of the Cuban Republic. Even under one phase of Mr. Dana's view, neutrality should have been declared, because the killing of American citizens, the imprisonment of others, the destruction of millions of dollars' worth of their property, and also the extensive commerce between Cuba and this nation, created such a "necessity" as not only demanded neutrality but justified intervention.

Spain's efforts to repress the rebellion are not the mere ordinary governmental agencies for the arrest and punishment of infractors of the law and which are supplemented by the posse comitatus; they are not the mere dispersal of a mob or the overthow of a multitude engaged in riotous demonstrations in which Spain is engaged; but a superhuman, death-like struggle of the military forces of the nation to prevent the complete extinguishment of the civil power within her chief province.

This, then, is "war in fact." And this position becomes impregnable when fortified by facts showing that the Cuban forces are not mere nomadic bands of unorganized malcontents, but are a powerful military organization, based upon organic law and subject to civil jurisdiction, occupying extensive territory and opposing successfully the vast military forces of the parent government. And, in addition, they are supported morally, financially, and otherwise by four-fifths of the inhabitants of their country.

The insurgents more than answer the requirements of Mr. Canning, the great English statesman, who said, when considering the case of the Greek revolutionists, that the character of belligerency is not so much a principle as a fact, and—

> That a certain degree of force and consistency acquired by a mass of population engaged in war entitled that population to be treated as belligerents. Even if their right was questionable, * * * it was the interest of nations, well understood, to so treat them.

In the struggle between conflicting forces in Mexico we recognized the government of Juarez as the rightful one, but treated both parties to the struggle as belligerents.

Ortolan contends that it is the general practice of nations to regard it a civil war when a considerable part of the citizens are proceeding with and against force to change or modify the government or to accomplish some other political design. (Volume 2, page 10, Dip. de la Mur.)

And Martens and Kluber declare it to be the duty of nations to assume neutrality, except when bound by treaties of alliance either offensive or defensive, with one of the belligerents.

Because the Spanish generals refuse flags of truce, or the exchange of prisoners, and ruthlessly butcher captured insurgents, is not a persuasive argument against affirmative action by us; and yet this savagery is assigned by the President, quoting from Grant, as one of the reasons why belligerency should not be granted. The history of the war proves that the insurgents treated prisoners in that humane manner required by international rules, and sought to conform to recognized usages of war.

In order to deprive them of the advantages of belligerency, which would result if Spain conducted the contest according to approved methods of warfare, she, both by civil and military authorities, insists that the Cubans are traitors and criminals (instead of political offenders), and treats them as such. But even applying the tests suggested by the President, belligerency long since should have been granted. There is a civil government, a de facto political organization. It has won to its support sufficient numerical strength to arm and equip and maintain in the field for nearly three years more than 30,000 soldiers.

A constitution has been adopted, liberal in its terms. Civil and military operations are conducted pursuant to its provisions. Officers are elected, laws are enacted, revenue is collected, a postal system is maintained, diplomatic agents appointed, a capital established, and the military forces have acted, so far as the parent government would permit, in harmony with the established rules of war. If Spain refused an exchange of prisoners, or to recognize flags of truce, the wrong, if it be one, must be visited upon the offender, not the innocent one. What more in justice and reason can be required by this Government before assuming neutrality?

It is a matter of history that many adventuresome sons of our Republic have supported in this contest the flag of Cuba. If captured by Spain, they are to be treated as traitors and malefactors. We accord them the same treatment because we deny them belligerency. The officials of this nation, Congress and the President, are indicted for conspiring with Spain to exterminate the noncombatants by starvation and hang the insurgents in arms as traitors. In the court of public conscience an impartial jury have pronounced the defendants guilty. What shall be the sentence?

The gentleman from Illinois [Mr. HITT] contended, and that view is taken by the President in his message, that belligerency would be disadvantageous to the insurgents. This is so fallacious, if not preposterous, that its advocacy is amazing. Why do the insurgents desire belligerent rights? Why is Spain unwilling that they shall be accorded if no benefits will result to the revolutionists? The present vice-president of the Cuban Republic, Salvador Cisneros, on the 1st of February, 1896, when he was president, addressed an eloquent appeal to the American people. He asked that international standing be given the insurgents and that—

The American people grant to us, through their President and Congress, those rights of belligerency to which, according to the laws of war and of nations, we are entitled. * * * Must we capture Habana and drive Spain's hirelings across the sea before we are even given the right of men to fight for that priceless gift which God destined should be universally divided among His children? Must we gain our independence before we are accorded the sanction of the world to labor for it? * * * Here in Cubitas are the head offices and chief departments of the republic; here we are able and most willing to receive representatives of the United States or other nations. * * * All we wish now is to be looked upon by the Government of the United States as men and soldiers battling for their birthright. We do not wish to appear in the eyes of the world like bandits and rabble.

And from that time until the present, able and distinguished representatives of the Republic of Cuba have been pleading with this nation to grant the prayer so eloquently offered by the first president of the republic. Some of the advantages accruing from a grant of belligerency, were pointed out by the able gentleman from Illinois when he was championing the cause of Cuba.

On April 3, 1896, when urging the House to pass the Senate resolution, he said:

Now, to answer the gentleman from Iowa, the effect of recognizing the belligerency of the Cubans will be, first, to give them a flag an l status. If a ship should enter New York Harbor this afternoon belonging to Cuban insurgents flying the lone star flag, she would be liable to be treated as a pirate and all on board might be treated as criminals, as violators of law, as enemies of mankind. With recognition, the belligerents will have a flag with the same status as that of any other country, and a vessel flying that flag can go into New York Harbor right alongside a Spanish frigate. But as we stand now, if they should go in this afternoon, the Spanish minister would be at the State Department immediately asking to have them seized and treated as pirates.

* * * After we have recognized the belligerent rights of the Cubans, men can openly leave our shores and aid the Cubans. The Cubans can go upon the stock boards in this city or anywhere else and publicly offer a loan—offer to negotiate their bonds as our fathers did during the Revolution at Amsterdam. They can negotiate loans either with other governments or with private citizens.

He then quotes the words of Minister Canovas, who said:

From the moment of their recognition they can send out vessels upon the ocean under the flag of the lone star, raise funds in foreign countries, move about with a freedom which was otherwise never enjoyed, and they could even carry on privateering.

And then the gentleman from Illinois proceeds:

That does not state all that the recognition of belligerency would accomplish; but it states the great and important advantages that such an act would give to the Cubans. * * * Why, sir, the United States is at this hour a base of operations of the Spanish Government in crushing the Cubans who are struggling for their freedom. Under the pretense of neutrality, we are, every time the Spanish minister gives information to the State Department, running to capture men who are about to start to Cuba or to seize supplies of arms intended for the Cubans. * * * We have not even confined our assistance to our own ports. In the case of the *Hawkins* we have pursued the Cubans out upon the high seas at the behest of Spain. Is that real neutrality? Is that fairness? Is it justice? Are we not in spirit and in fact the efficient oppressors of the Cubans ourselves?

Those strong, fearless words came from the gentleman when he was sympathizing with the Cubans, and contending that their independence would result by granting belligerency. Now he seeks to darken our councils; the spell of the President's message has fallen upon him. We have been insisting that this Government should neither in spirit nor in fact be the efficient oppressors of the Cubans, but that its heavy hand should be taken from them, that they might be permitted in their own way to fight their battles for freedom, receiving at our hands only the same treatment which we accord to their oppressors.

When the Spanish minister demanded of President Madison that our ports be closed against the flags of revolting colonies in South America, the President, through Monroe, stated in effect that the demand could not be complied with; that "each party was permitted to enter our ports with its public and private ships and take from them every article which was the subject of commerce with other nations."

In Mr. Dana's edition of Wheaton (page 34 and note) the following language was used:

They [insurgents] gain a great advantage of recognized status and the opportunity to employ commissioned cruisers at sea and to exert all the power known to maritime warfare with the sanction of foreign nations. They can obtain abroad loans, military and naval materials, and enlist men as against everything but neutrality laws. Their flag and commissions are acknowledged, their revenue laws respected, and they acquire a quasi-political recognition.

Justice Brown, in the Abrose-Light Case (25 Fed. Rep., 418), says that—

The recognition by at least some established government of a state of war, or of the belligerent rights of insurgents, is necessary to prevent their cruisers from being held legally piratical by the courts of other nations injuriously affected, is either directly confirmed or necessarily implied from many adjudged cases.

From these and many other authorities to which reference might be made it is patent that great advantages to the Cuban insurgents would have been derived from such recognition. Loans would have been negotiated, privateering conducted, munitions of war purchased from us, thousands of our chivalrous and gallant sons recruited into the Cuban armies, and to-day Cuba would not be in desolation and ruin; but, with the bright flag of a virile, young nation, she would have entered upon the great highway trodden by progressive nations, acknowledging the beneficence of republican institutions and the glorious example established by our nation, the firstborn of the continent.

This duty unperformed, has pressed upon us other and important ones. The Cubans will achieve their independence whether we recognize them as belligerents or not, or whether there is any intervention by us in their behalf. What Chatham said of our fathers is true of the Cubans:

You can not conquer America. You may raise armies, you may make campaigns, you may even win battles, but you will never subdue the spirit of liberty in that people.

If there is no recognition of independence, there should be belligerency.

By granting belligerency it would hasten Cuban independence; but the cruelties and sorrows and horrors of the situation would continue, our commerce still further suffer, our peace as a nation would be disturbed, and the interests of our people and Government rendered still more insecure. To prevent the continuation of this great crime against humanity, this desolation, ruin, and death, the United States should immediately recognize the independence of the Cuban Republic, enter into diplomatic relations with it, compel a suspension of hostilities so that the murder of the reconcentrados might cease, then mediate to secure Spain's abandonment of the contest and the relinquishment of her authority therein.

If the Cuban people were willing to pay to Spain a monetary consideration for the complete extinguishment of her sovereignty, it would be a matter in which our voice would be silent. If Spain perversely refused such mediation, and continued the work of devastation and death, by force, cooperating with the Cuban armies, this nation should drive her flag from Cuban soil, and join in the coronation of a new government—this isle of the free, this home of the brave.

International law supports this position, and our peculiar relations to Cuba, together with the occurrences of the century which affect Spain, Cuba, and the United States, multiply the reasons justifying it. Before discussing the legal aspect of the question involved in the proposition of intervention, I desire to invite attention to some historic facts demonstrating that Spain has forfeited all right to the possession or control of Cuba.

We have passed from the gloom and darkness of mediævalism, but Spain has refused to accept the inspiration prophetic of a truer civilization and a glorified era. Her conquests have been by the sword and the power of might; justice and mercy have been unknown quantities in her foreign administration. The New World was prostrate at her feet. Instead of seeking the enlightenment of its inoffensive children and the establishment of colonial governments intrenched in the affections of the people, she sought their destruction, and, with the utmost ferocity, despoiled them of place and nation. Cupidity and avarice intensified their brutality.

Two purposes only guided Spain in dealing with her colonies in the New World. First, to enrich the parent Government by their exploitation and the enforced sale of Spanish products to the Cuban people. Second, their political control by an oligarchy, in order to furnish places and offices for hordes of Spanish courtiers and satellites. There was no attempt to advance the material interests of the colonies and their people or to bring about industrial development. The most repressive measures were adopted to prevent political independence or financial growth, which might lead to discontent toward parent State.

The same policy which Tacitus informs us Rome applied to Great Britain, that of plundering and of enslaving the people, was regarded as the proper one to control the colonial dependencies. To the colonies no form of local self-government was given. Officials were sent by the Crown armed with despotic power. They ruled without law, except their own tyrannous will. Civil law was a figment, personal rights and liberty were unknown. There could only be in time one result of this imperialism. Revolts and revolutions succeeded each other. Made desperate by the outrages and wrongs perpetrated upon succeeding generations, the spirit of determined resistance seized the people, and the yoke of Spain was thrown off.

The South American colonies under Boliver, San Martin, O'Higgins, and other valorous leaders, won their independence. Mexico and the Central American States followed their example, until at last in the empires possessed by Spain in the New World, only "the ever-faithful isle" and Puerto Rico remained. Her misfortunes in the government of her colonies and the humiliating defeats sustained at their hands have wrought no change in her system of administering Cuban affairs.

During the century her anger has been kindled against Cuba, and she has enforced her paternalistic policy and more fully developed the commercial system which makes Cuba a tributary to Spain. She destroyed the vast population inhabiting the island at the time of its discovery, and then planted the system of slavery. When, through the force of revolution, she was compelled to abandon slavery. she sought Asiatic importations to found another condition of servitude. She has sent Governors-General who were so corrupt and despotic that almost "all had to be deposed and dispelled. Some, such as Gaspar de Torres, were real highwaymen." (Dic. Enc. Hisp., page 1467.)

These men by decree of May 28, 1825, had—

The fullest authority, the same powers being bestowed which by the royal ordinances are granted to the governors of besieged cities. In consequence of this His Majesty gives * * * the most ample and unbounded power, not only to send away from the island any persons in office, whatever their occupation, rank, class, or condition, whose continuance therein * * * may be deemed injurious (by the Governor-General) or whose condu t, public or private, may alarm you, * * * but also to suspend the execution of any order whatsoever or any general provision made concerning any branch of the administration as may be thought most suitable to the royal service.

Because Spain has denied Cubans a participation in the government of their own affairs and condemned them to political inferiority in the land of their birth, because she confiscates the product of their labor, impoverishes the people, deprives them of sacred and dear rights, maintains a despotic militarism, and compels the acceptance of a Spanish bureaucracy, the Cubans have again and again appealed for redress. Entreaties have been unavailing. Insurrections and revolutions have then followed. So that the century presents a pathetic picture—Cuba despoiled and plundered; Spain profiting by her misfortunes; the oppressed pleading for liberty and a mitigation of their sorrow; Spain coquetting with their demands, promising relief only to find pretexts for denying righteous demands; revolutions, carnage, and bloodshed; and the chapter is not yet closed.

The revolutions of 1850 and 1851 were speedily overthrown, but in 1855 the Cubans conspired again for independence. In 1868 the conflict began and raged for ten years. On the 24th of February, 1895, men who accepted peace in 1878 again joined the standard of revolt and, with their sons, fight on for liberty, home, and country.

During the ten years' war the property of many of the Cubans was confiscated and the country laid waste; yet upon the establishment of peace, Spain's exactions reached the enormous figure of $46,000,000 for the fiscal year 1879. It was slightly reduced in 1883, and since 1886 the annual budget has been fixed at about $26,000,000.

With this enormous drain upon the island, and with repressive and restrictive legislation, in the interests of Catalonia and important manufacturing and producing cities of Spain, (which were barriers to the commercial nations with which Cuba desired to deal and by natural laws were her proper and natural markets of trade); it becomes a matter of wonder that the people could meet these demands and still give to the island a value of nearly $1,000,000,000 before the present war overwhelmed it.

The capacity of the people to bear these great burdens testifies eloquently to their industry, and is strong evidence of their ability for self-government. And it is conceded by Spanish authority that there must be added to this large sum annually taken to replenish the coffers of Spain, millions of dollars which, by peculation and malversation in office, were diverted from the revenue channels by the Spanish bureaucracy.

Señor Roblado, the present leader of the Conservatives in Spain, stated in the Cortes May 28, 1890, speaking of the the defalcation of the Spanish officials in Cuba:

They amount to the following sum: 22,811,516 pesetas. Did not the Government know this? What has been done?

And Señor Castaneda stated in the Spanish Cortes June 24, 1891:

How can any one doubt that corruption exists in the Island of Cuba? General Prendergast has furnished a list of 359 persons employed in the custom-houses against whom proceedings have been taken for fraud, and not one of them has been punished.

Señor Dolz, a Spanish deputy, published in the Atenebo de Madrid, in the spring of 1895, a statement that the custom-house frauds in Cuba since the year 1877 amounted to $100,000,000.

Captain-General Dulce, writing to the minister for the colonies in 1867, said:

The cause of trouble and of the inquietude which appears in the island of Cuba should be sought for to a great extent in the tariff laws, which, under the pretext of protection, make impossible a commerce carried on in good faith. * * * The custom-house system is very expensive, overloaded with formalities, which do not prevent fraud, but which embarrass and annoy honest trade. The ordinance of matriculas, instead of protecting industry upon the seas, has well-nigh destroyed it.

The debate in the Spanish Cortes in June, 1890, revealed that a perfect saturnalia of larceny and corruption existed in the custom-houses and various other departments provided for the collection of revenues in Cuba. The minister of the colonies, residing at Madrid, has nearly $100,000 annually assigned to him; the governor-general, $50,000 annually, in addition to palaces and expenses of maintaining his household; the director-general of the treasury, $18,000 per annum; the archbishop of Santiago and the bishop of Habana, $18,000 each; and so on ad infinitum. General Pando, in March, 1890, affirmed that the board of public debt had committed robberies exceeding the sum of $12,000,000.

By the venal methods employed by these swarms of Spanish officeholders controlling Cuba, it has been said that from one-fourth to one-half of all revenues collected are embezzled. The debt of Cuba in 1868 was $25,000,000. By the scandalous, immoral fiscal system imposed by Spain since that time, this indebtedness in 1895 had reached the fabulous sum of nearly $300,000,000. This debt was created by Spain, not Cuba. The Cubans had no voice in obtaining the money, nor were they consulted in the expenditure of it.

More than five hundred millions in addition to this sum, between the close of the ten-years war and the commencement of hostilities, have been wrung from the island. This amount went to replenish Spain's exhausted treasury and to meet advances made in the Carlist wars and her controversies in Santo Domingo and Peru. None of it went for the upbuilding of Cuba. No schools were established, no highways built, no public improvements made.

In the budget of 1895, which appropriated and distributed over $26,000,000, only $746,925 was ostensibly appropriated for local improvements. I sought in vain when in Cuba for any evidences of a just or beneficent administration by the Peninsula. It is a fact beyond question that Spain has exploited the Cubans and delivered them over to be plundered by corrupt, venal, impecunious camp followers of the Spanish Crown and its satellites. I found no schools, no highways, no improved harbors, no asylums—none of those evidences which mark a judicious application of public revenues. Spain was warned of this unnatural and despotic course. In the Cortes in 1866 a deputy said:

I foresee a catastrophe near at hand in case Spain persists in remaining deaf to the just reclamations of the Cubans. Look at the old colonies of the

3223

American continent. All have ended in conquering their independence. Let Spain not forget the lesson; let the Government be just to the colonies that remain. Thus she will consolidate her dominion over people who only aspire to be good sons of a worthy mother, but who are not willing to live as slaves under the scepter of a tyrant.

These evils becoming unbearable, a declaration of independence was issued October 10, 1868, at Yara, and Cespedes, with 128 ill-armed men, raised the standard of revolution. Some of the grievances alluded to are stated in the declaration as follows:

And as Spain has many a time promised us Cubans to respect our rights without having hitherto fulfilled her promises; as she continues to tax us heavily, and by so doing is likely to destroy our wealth; as we are in danger of losing our property, our lives, and our honor, under further Spanish dominion, etc.

It is not my purpose to detail the sorrowful, sickening proceedings of this conflict, of the cruelties and barbarities perpetrated by Valmaceda, Weyler, and other Spanish commanders and officials, or to dwell on the long, sanguinary struggle which resulted in the loss of over 100,000 Spanish troops through sickness, disease, and war, and the destruction of thousands of Cubans and the desolation of a large portion of the island.

At last General Campos, commanding the Spanish armies, negotiated with the Cuban leaders for the establishment of peace, and in February, 1878, articles of peace were agreed upon. Indubitable proofs exist that Spain has flagrantly violated the terms of that treaty, and that the present revolution is directly caused by her perfidy and the continuous oppression of her Cuban subjects.

Señor Maura, who was minister for the colonies in 1893, offered a measure of colonial reform containing many admirable, liberal features. It partially met the requirements of the peace of Zanjon.

It was quickly defeated in the Cortes, and Señor Barbazuza prepared a colonial scheme of government which was approved by the Cortes in February, 1895. It was not real or genuine, and gave neither administrative decentralization nor political or industrial relief to the Cubans. It maintained the same paternalism, perpetuated the same monopoly of trade in favor of Spain, by means of differential duties and obstructions to commercial relations with the United States and other nations.

It still converted the island into a prey for the Spanish vampires and officeholders, and condemned the Cubans to the same slavery and inequality so long endured. The news of this mockery quickly reached the island, and on the 24th of February the fires of revolution were lighted.

Vattel announces that promises and conventions must be respected by rulers and governments, and when broken revolution is justifiable.

Promises of genuine autonomy and the abolition of the obnoxious colonial system prevailing, brought the peace of Zanjon; but no effort was made, except as above stated, to effect the promised reforms.

General Campos wrote a year thereafter, a letter which shows the duplicity of Spain. It was read in the Spanish Senate by Canovas July 21, 1879:

Promises never fulfilled, abuses of all kinds, no provision made for agriculture and public works, the exclusion of the natives from all branches of the administration, and other faults implanted gave rise to the insurrection of Yara. The conviction of successive governments, that no other means can be used here but terror, and that it is a matter of dignity not to begin reform as long as a shot is fired, may be continued. If we do not wish to ruin Spain, we must take up frankly the question of liberty.

The Madrid Liga Heraria of July 27, 1879, in publishing this, then asks:

What have we done from the peace of Zanjon to this day to prevent a repetition of what happened at Yara?

The eminent Spanish statesman, Pei y Margall, said, as quoted in the Madrid Don Qui Jote, July 12, 1879:

We must endeavor to reestablish the principles of justice. No nation has the right to occupy other territory inhabited by other men unless with their consent. * * * No prescription is possible in this matter. Prescription does not apply and never does apply to the right of liberty and independence. * * * Let us make them masters and arbiters of their own destinies. Let us leave them to rule themselves in all matters pertaining to their internal life, political, administrative, and economic.

* * * Against such conduct the sentiment of patriotism is invoked. But above the idea of country arises that of humanity, and above both that of justice. Cuba is the grave of our youth in these deplorable wars. Our soldiers perish there by thousands. * * * The greater part is dragged there by force and must fight for a cause that is distasteful to them. * * * Must the nation to be sovereign drain the life of the groups composing it? Does its sovereignty necessarily carry with it the slavery of colonies?

The statement of one of our own consuls, as reported by the State Department in 1885, proves the intolerable condition of the Spanish dominion:

The entire population with the exception of the official class are living under a tyranny unparalleled at this day on the globe. There is a system of oppression and torture which enters every phase of life, eats into the soul of every Cuban, mortifies, injures, and insults him every hour, impoverishes him and his family from day to day, threatens the rich man with bankruptcy and the poor man with beggary. The exactions of the Spanish Government and the illegal outrages of its officers are in fact intolerable. They have reduced the islands to despondency and ruin. * * * The Government at Madrid is directly answerable for the misery of Cuba and for the rapacity and venality of its subordinates. * * * A war tax of the most exaggerated character was laid. Every business, trade, art, or profession is taxed in the proportion of 25 to 33⅓ per cent of its net income. * * * All the petty trades and employments in the country are separately suffering. All participate in the common distress.

Between the peace of Zanjon and the breaking out of the present war it was apparent to the Cubans no amelioration of their condition was possible except such as was gained by the sword. Taxes had been levied anew on everything, the offices were still filled by Spaniards, the professed extension of suffrage to the Cubans was rendered inoperative by Spanish administration, malversation and the most flagrant frauds were still perpetrated in the revenue and other departments, representation was denied, the public revenues applied exclusively to pay Spanish debts and to maintain the army and navy, and the industrial depression, by these vicious means and discriminatory legislation, had become so acute that stagnation in business and an economic and monetary crisis resulted. A revolution was the only fruit possible upon this upas tree of Spain's planting.

José Marti established a provisional, independent government, which has successfully maintained itself against the power of Spain until the present hour. So vigorous were its military operations, that the magnanimous Campos was hurriedly recalled to Spain, and the unmentionable Weyler sent to succeed him. Then followed a reign of terror and bloodshed so horrible as to defy description.

None in Cuba deny these inhuman acts attributed to him. The Spanish people admit them, and the evidences of their perpetration are incontestable. The proclamations of Valmaceda in the ten years' war, that—

all persons captured in Spanish waters or on the high seas near Cuba, no matter their derivation or destination, having arms or munitions aboard,

8223

are to be treated as pirates and immediately executed, and every habitation unoccupied will be burned by the troops, and those from which a white flag does not float reduced to ashes, and every man over 15 years of age found away from his habitation failing to prove a justifiable motive shall be shot—

were not more cruel. Against that mode of warfare Mr. Fish, at the direction of President Grant, protested:

The order to indiscriminately slaughter all persons captured in such vessel, without regard to their number, could not but shock the sensibilities of all humane persons.

Mr. Fish further stated:

In the interest of Christian civilization and common humanity, I hope this document is a forgery. If it be indeed genuine, the President instructs me in the most forcible manner to protest against such a mode of warfare and to ask you to request the Spanish authorities in Cuba to take such steps as no person having the right to proclaim the protection of the Government of the United States shall be sacrificed or injured in the conduct of hostilities upon this basis.

Under Weyler's orders pacificos and noncombatants were slaughtered, Cabanas fortress and other prisons filled with innocent men and women, many of whom were never heard of again, the homes and property of the Cubans in the four western provinces of the island destroyed by the torch in the hands of the Spanish soldiers and guerrillas, and the helpless, homeless people, more than half a million in number, forced into fortified cities and towns, there to become victims of starvation and the ravages of diseases produced by their privations and suffering.

This is a brief recital of Spain's record in Cuba. Are her crimes and savagery to be endured forever? In the words of Margall, "Above country is humanity, and above both is justice." Justice has pronounced judgment. Spain has forfeited all right to further interest in Cuba.

While this record was being made, how has her conduct affected this Government and its interests?

Our commerce with Cuba, aggregating nearly $100,000,000 per annum, has been practically destroyed; American citizens have been ruthlessly butchered, and property belonging to American citizens which exceeded $50,000,000 in value has been rendered worthless; hundreds of American citizens have been made beggars and are now wandering in the streets of Cuban cities, homeless and dependent upon the charity of this Government; between three and four hundred thousand people have met wretched deaths as reconcentrados and noncombatants; 200,000 still more wretched Cubans are now unprovided for, and will, in the event of the prolongation of the struggle in its present form, soon meet the same fate; 25,000 Cubans, fearing imprisonment or death for alleged political offenses, are refugees within our own borders. Our ears and eyes have been witnesses for nearly three years of this most horrible condition; we have constantly been importuned from all quarters to interpose, to prevent the continuation of this awful carnival; the peace of our nation has been during this long period disturbed and the interests of our nation menaced; the sensibilities of the people have been shocked, and all have joined in solemnly protesting against this great crime against humanity.

All these things have profoundly impressed the American people, and they believe that, measured by any moral or ethical code or any divine or human law, national or international, a period has been reached when we ought not to be required to suffer longer or endure further this awful spectacle. And the additional reasons must not be forgotten. We are employing an arm of our

3238

naval power in guarding the high seas in the interest of Spain. This tax is becoming burdensome.

It is not only during this revolution that we have been compelled to suffer from the conditions in Cuba. The numerous insurrections and wars extending over the century have been an unceasing source of trouble, irritation, expense, anxiety, and sorrow to our nation and people. And during much of this period our relations with Spain have been delicate and strained.

She has impressed our seamen, disregarded treaty obligations, and, in the case of the *Virginius*, executed American citizens.

The State Department contains voluminous reports containing protests, demands, explanations, negotiations, and all of the petty wretched circumlocution incident to diplomatic conduct. This nation has been patient, but the hour has now arrived when a firm, vigorous American policy should be pursued. France, it is suggested, may interfere in this matter. Spanish bonds have procured French money, and French influences are operating to bring to a close this contest with victory to Spain.

If for any consideration we are restrained from now acting, and if the insurgents are vanquished, what assurances are there that within less than a decade a reenactment of the same scenes and crimes would not occur? Spain of to-morrow will be the Spain of to-day and yesterday, applying the same methods, exercising the same despotism; and the Cubans of the future will be as the Cubans of the past, with this difference, that each year and each day the glory of our nation's freedom will give added strength to their purpose to gain that which we enjoy.

The Cuban question never can be and never will be settled, and our peace ever will be disturbed, until the scepter of Spain's power passes forever from Cuba's shore. When Amelia Island was the rendezvous of buccaneers and those whose predatory incursions injured our commerce and disturbed our peace, our ships were sent to drive them from the island, though it was a Spanish possession. The condition amounted in law to a nuisance, and we abated it.

If a strong man is constantly and cruelly wounding his child, and a person is so situate as to be the enforced witness of the crime, human law, receiving moral sanction, approves the effort to arrest the parent's misconduct.

In addition to our material and commercial interests in the island, there is an abiding one founded upon affinity if not consanguinity. Washington when President said:

Born, sir, in a land of liberty; having early learned its value; having engaged in a perilous conflict to defend it; having, in a word, devoted the best years of my life to secure its permanent establishment in my own country, my anxious recollections, my sympathetic feelings, and my best wishes are irresistibly excited whensoever in any country I see an oppressed nation unfurl the banners of freedom.

The words of Webster are a command to us in this hour of vacillation and neglected duty. When pleading for the recognition of Grecian independence in the House of Representatives in 1823, he used these words:

What part it becomes this country to take on a question of this sort, so far as it is called upon to take any part, can not be doubtful. Our side of this question is settled for us even without our own volition. Our history, our situation, our character, necessarily decide our position and our course before we have even time to ask whether we have an option. Our place is on the side of free institutions.

And in his masterly letter to Mr. Hulsemann, in answer to the latter's communication remonstrating, in behalf of the Austrian

Government, against the action of the President (in sending Mr. Clayton to ascertain the progress of the Hungarian revolution) and certain expressions used by the President, Mr. Webster states:

> And if the United States wish success to countries contending for popular institutions and national independence, it is only because they regard such constitutions and such national independence not as imaginary, but real justice. * * * When the United States behold the people of foreign countries without any such interference spontaneously moving forward for the adoption of institutions like their own, it surely can not be expected of them to remain wholly indifferent spectators.

Mr. Fish, in his memorable letter to Mr. Cushing, under date of November 5, 1875, said:

> While remembering and observing the duties which this Government as one of the family of nations owes to another member by public law, treaties, or the particular statutes of the United States, it would be idle to attempt to conceal the interest and sympathy with which Americans in the United States regard any attempt of a numerous people on this continent to be relieved of ties which hold them in the position of colonial subjection to a distant power, and to assume the independence and the right of self-control which natural rights and the spirit of the age accord them.

Cuba has engaged the attention of American statesmen, and has been a matter of grave concern to our Presidents, for nearly a hundred years. The uncertain tenure of Spain's holding, and the oppressive colonial system maintained, as well as the disquietude constantly prevailing there, of necessity brought the subject prominently into view. And after the promulgation of the Monroe doctrine, and European nations sought an alliance with Monroe, by which Cuba was to be guaranteed as a possession of Spain, our concern in her welfare was increased.

The important position which it holds in commanding the Gulf, and its proximity to our shores, made the question of its ownership transcendently important. Monroe, taking counsel from Jefferson and other great statesmen, announced that no European power should be permitted to interfere with Cuba; that while Spain's claim would not be controverted, the acquisition by any other nation would not be tolerated. At the same time it was either directly or indirectly understood by American statesmen that ultimately Spain's supremacy would be lost.

European nations acquiesced in Monroe's position, so that our nation has been the voluntary, self-appointed guardian of Cuba. It is a national policy which forbids Cuba, no matter what her wrongs and oppressions may be at the hands of Spain, from securing European aid or contracting an alliance, offensive or defensive, with a European power. We prevent other nations from giving moral or material support to Cuba in revolutions provoked by Spanish oppression. Does it comport with decency or dignity or right for this nation, under such circumstances, to be an indifferent spectator to her woes and afflictions?

As early as 1823 the unrest in Cuba occasioned us solicitude. Jefferson, in writing to President Monroe, June 11, 1823, said:

> Cuba alone seems at present to hold up a speck of war to us.

And the letter of Mr. Adams, Secretary of State, to Minister Nelson, in the same year, evidenced the grave apprehension which Cuba, as a European dependency, created.

In 1825 Cuba again became an object of international negotiation. England desired a joint declaration by the Governments of the United States, France, and Great Britain to protect Spain's title to the island. It was hoped, if this step were taken, that an immediate acknowledgment would be made by Spain of the South

3223

American Republics. During the incumbency of Mr. Van Buren as Secretary of State, Cuba's relations with Spain and the United States were constantly discussed.

And in 1827 Mr. Everett complained of the connivance of the Spanish Crown with the British ministry and Spanish refugees who were inaugurating movements for the revolutionizing of the island. In 1830 additional complications arose, and shortly after we find the State Department again concerned in Cuba's peace, and prospective European combinations which it was considered would imperil our nation. In 1851, Mr. Webster, then Secretary of State, in a communication to Mr. Barringer, shows the interest of the United States in Cuba and the troubles occasioned the former in suppressing invasions calculated to overthrow Spain's power in the island. In 1852, when Mr. Everett was Secretary of State, we find him occupied in dealing with the Cuban question. He states:

> The United States, on the other hand, would by the proposed convention disable themselves from making an acquisition which might take place without any disturbance of existing foreign relations and in the natural order of things. The Island of Cuba lies at our doors. It commands the approach to the Gulf of Mexico, which washes the shores of five of our States. It bars the entrance of that great river which drains half the North American continent and with its tributaries forms the largest system of internal water communication in the world. It keeps watch at the doorway of our intercourse with California by the Isthmus route. If an island like Cuba, belonging to the Spanish Crown, guarded the entrance of the Thames and the Seine, and the United States should propose a convention like this to France and England, those powers would assuredly feel that the disability assumed by ourselves was far less serious than that which we ask them to assume. The opinions of American statesmen at different times and under varying circumstances have differed as to the desirableness of the acquisition of Cuba by the United States. Territorially and commercially it would in our hands be an extremely valuable possession. Under certain contingencies it might be almost essential to our safety.

And on the 3d of December of the same year he wrote to Mr. Crampton as follows:

> To enter into a compact with European powers to the effect that the United States as well as the other contracting powers—

Referring to England and France— •

> would disclaim all intentions now or hereafter to obtain possession of Cuba would be inconsistent with the principle, the policy, and the tradition of the United States.

President Fillmore in his message of 1852 referred to the uneasy condition and feeling of alarm on the part of the Cuban authorities. He complained of the interference by the Spanish officials with our commercial intercourse with the island. Cuba continued to be a source of irritation to the United States, and was the prolific cause of many state papers by Mr. Marcy and other officials of our Government.

President Buchanan in his message (1858) states:

> The truth is that Cuba, in its existing colonial condition, is a constant source of annoyance to the American people. * * * With that island under the dominion of a distant foreign power, this trade—

From the Mississippi River in the United States—

> of vital importance to these States, is exposed to the danger of being destroyed in time of war, and it has hitherto been subjected to perpetual injury and annoyance in time of peace. Our relations with Spain, which ought to be of the most friendly character, must always be placed in jeopardy while the existing colonial government over the island shall remain in its present condition.

In 1869 President Grant's first annual message discusses at some length the Cuban question, and calls attention to the fact that for more than a year a revolution has been waged in the island for independence and freedom. He refers to the effort of the United

States to bring the contest to a termination and stop the blood-shed occasioned by the revolution.

In his special message of June 13, 1870, reference is made to the destruction of property belonging to American citizens and the imprisonment of some and the sacrifice of the lives of others. In his message the following year he complains of the disturbed condition of the island and the great concern, annoyance, and anxiety resulting therefrom.

The able Secretary of State, Mr. Fish, on October 29, 1872, in writing to Mr. Sickles, our minister at Madrid, referred to the ineffectual efforts of Spain to suppress the insurrection, the destruction of life and property, and the great commercial and other connections existing between the United States and the island. He also complained of the great strain imposed upon the United States in enforcing the neutrality laws, and intimated that if Spain's inability to establish peace should long continue the commercial interests of the people of the United States, as well as the Government's duty to itself, might require the adoption of a different policy.

In writing to Mr. Cushing, February 6, 1874, he states:

> Civil dissensions in Cuba and especially sanguinary hostilities, such as are now raging there, produce effects in the United States second in gravity only to those which they produce in Spain. * * * Meanwhile this condition of things grows day by day more and more insupportable to the United States. The Government is compelled to exert constantly the utmost vigilance to prevent infringement of our law on the part of Cubans purchasing munitions or materials of war or laboring to fit out military expeditions in our ports; we are constrained to maintain a large naval force to prevent violations of our sovereignty either by the Cubans or by the Spaniards; our people are horrified and agitated at the spectacle at our very doors of war not only with all its ordinary attendance of devastation and carnage, but with the accompaniments of barbarous shooting of prisoners of war, or their summary execution by military commission, to the scandal and disgrace of the age; we are under the necessity of interposing continually for the protection of our citizens against wrongful acts of local authorities of Spain in Cuba; and the public peace is every moment subject to be interrupted by some unforeseen event, like that which recently occurred to drive us at once to the brink of war with Spain. In short, the state of Cuba is the one great cause of perpetual solicitude in the foreign relations of the United States.

In President Grant's seventh annual message attention is directed to the protracted strife in Cuba, to the extent of seriously crippling commercial nations, especially the United States, and to the loss of property by the citizens of the United States. Almost the first act of President Hayes was to direct the attention of Congress to the baneful effects upon the United States of the hostilities in Cuba, and the unlawful proceedings of Spain in interfering with American vessels and commerce in making illegal arrests and levying oppressive taxes upon American residents.

President Arthur did not escape a question which had challenged most of his predecessors, and we find him in 1884, in his message to Congress, alluding to the neutrality laws and the vigilance required upon the part of the United States to prevent infractions by persons who were endeavoring to bring about a revolt in Cuba against Spanish authority.

Mr. Cleveland was compelled to deal with the unpleasant heritage. On December 7. 1896, in addressing Congress, he referred to the interests of the United States in Cuba, the commercial relations between them, the capital invested in railroads, mines, and other enterprises, and argued that the United States "are inextricably involved in the controversy in other ways, both vexatious and costly," and that the struggle which was ruining the island was of serious concern to our people, and that our interests were not "wholly sentimental or philanthropic."

The present Executive is confronted with the same question, but a crisis has now been reached. All the currents of the past are converged and there must be a solution of the question.

It is a litigated question which has been in the court of public conscience for nearly a hundred years and international forums for three-quarters of a century. The court of final resort has now been reached.

President McKinley denominates the issues as the—

most important problem with which this Government is now called upon to deal pertaining to its foreign relations.

For no enduring period since the enfranchisement of the continental possessions of Spain in the Western Continent has the condition of Cuba or the policy of Spain toward Cuba not caused concern to the United States. * * * The existing conditions can not but fill this Government and the American people with the gravest apprehension.

Such a record as this is conclusive proof that the safety and welfare of this nation, its peace and honor, its commercial interests, and the protection of its citizens having property interests in Cuba can only be preserved and secured by the termination of Spanish supremacy in Cuba. We can no longer be required to maintain an "expectant attitude," waiting for Spain to adopt a proper colonial policy, to deal righteously with the Cuban people, and to reestablish an honorable, just, and lasting peace with her revolted subjects. What, then, is the remedy? In my opinion, it lies in intervention by the United States. Spain has been repeatedly warned for seventy-five years that the United States could not forever behold the lamentable conditions prevailing in Cuba and the prospect of continued revolutions so distracting to our peace and injurious to this nation.

Examples are numerous in history of intervention by governments in the affairs of others. Whatever high and worthy reasons have existed as authority for interfering in the political concerns of nations, whatever sanction such interference may have found in international law, all can now be invoked in justification of direct, immediate, and, if necessary, armed intervention by this nation to free the lamb from the vulture's clutches, to release the innocent, struggling child from the grasp of the inhuman, debased, and barbarous parent.

The grounds assigned for intervention have been various. The following have been regarded as sufficient to warrant it: "Impediments to commerce," "Burdensome measures of protection and repression," "Effusion of blood," "Humanity," and "The repose of Europe." England and other powers intervened in the case of Belgium in 1830 because of "a warm desire to arrest, with the shortest possible delay, the disorder and the effusion of blood."

Under the treaty of Berlin in 1878, intervention in behalf of Servia, Roumania, Montenegro, and Bulgaria was predicated upon the ground of a "desire to regulate." Humanitarian feelings prompted intervention in 1827 by Great Britain, France, and Russia in behalf of the Greek revolutionists. The religious persecutions inflicted by the Sultan of Turkey and the policy of extermination pursued by the Ottoman Government aroused the Greeks to heroic and desperate resistance. Owing to the timely aid afforded by the great powers they achieved independence.

Speaking of this contest, Dr. Wheaton states that—

The rights of human nature wantonly outraged by this cruel warfare were but tardily and imperfectly vindicated by this measure, but its principl̃ was fully justified by the great, paramount law of self-preservation. "Whatever a nation may lawfully defend for itself, it may defend for another if called on to interpose." This interference of the Christian powers to put an end to this bloody contest might safely, therefore, have been rested on this ground alone, without appealing to the interests of commerce and of the repose of Europe, which, as well as the interests of humanity, are alluded to in the treaty as the determining motives of the high contracting parties.

There is great contrariety of opinion expressed by publicists and international writers as to what grounds forcible intervention may rightfully be predicated upon, but all concede that as an act of self-defense, or for self-protection, it is permissible and fully authorized. While there is not complete harmony upon the part of the writers referred to as to the classification of the reasons assigned as justification, under the names of "order," "peace," and "commercial relations," as well as "property rights of citizens," still there is a substantial concurrence of expression that the protection of these interests rests upon the right of self-defense; and that for continued invasion of such interests, and the disturbance of such "peace," "order," and rights, forcible intervention is justifiable.

Whether forcible intervention is authorized upon humanitarian grounds alone is not free from doubt if determination rests upon the "weight of authority"—that is, of standard authors on international law. Slight consideration has been devoted to this important subject, and no established rules are deducible from the books. But certain it is there is a growing sentiment which will ultimately be crystallized into positive international rule—that brutal massacres, long-continued oppression, resulting in slavery, poverty, and destruction of property and life, wars of extermination and barbarous and despotic treatment without signs of cessation, which brutalize and degrade, will be sufficient warrant for intervention to prevent their continuance, at least when, by such crimes and oppressions by one government against a portion of its subjects, the moral sentiments of nations are shocked and their peace and quiet rendered insecure.

Vattel recognizes succor to people oppressed by their sovereign as proper. Logically, if the sovereign refuses the proffered succor, the interposing nation would have a right to compel acceptance.

Heffter denies the right of intervention for the repression of tyranny, but insists that if civil war results (because of oppression) between the sovereign and a portion of its subjects, then assistance by intervention or otherwise may be rendered in behalf of either party.

Calvo and Fiore contend for the right of intervention to put an end to crimes and slaughter.

Woolsey, in his most excellent treatise on International Law, justifies interference in the affairs of other states when it is demanded by self-preservation, and when some extraordinary state of things is brought about by the crime of a government against its subjects.

Under Dr. Wheaton's broad statement, quoted from McIntosh, "that whatever a nation may defend for itself it may defend for another," interference in Cuba is clearly warranted. Cuba's right of revolution is as sacred and as well grounded in the principles of right and justice as the Greeks'; and if the revolution rests upon the ground that a great crime was being committed, we have the right to recognize the government of the revolutionists and aid in the effort to prevent the continuance of such crime. Even Grotius admits that occasions may arise justifying resistance to the sover-

eign. The doctrine taught by Hobbes of patrimonial kingdoms
has passed away, like many of the exploded theories of the past.

Manning, in his Law of Nations, page 97, states as grounds on
which interference with the affairs of foreign states would now
be held capable of justification:

(2) The continuance of a revolutionary state of affairs in a foreign state
under circumstances in which it seems highly probable that without such
interference either public order can never be restored at all or can only be
restored after such sufferings to humanity and such injuries to surrounding
states as obviously overbalance the general evil of all interference from
without.

The other forms which interference may take are:

(3) Actual support of a revolutionary party in a foreign state, or of the
government of a state in its efforts to suppress a revolution; and (4) public
recognition for the purpose of general intercourse on equal terms of a newly
formed though perhaps not yet firmly established government.

Phillimore announces the following rule with respect to this
question:

The right of self-defense may, in certain cases, carry with it the necessity
of intervening in the relations and, to a certain extent, of controlling the
conduct of another state, and this when the interest of the intervenor is not
immediately and directly but mediately and indirectly affected.

He further states that in "self-defense" interference is justifiable "when the domestic institutions of a state are inconsistent
with the peace and safety of other states;" and also upon invitation of belligerent parties in a civil war.

Hall states the doctrine of intervention as follows:

The grounds upon which intervention has taken place or upon which it is
said with more or less of authority that it is permitted may be referred to
the right of self-preservation, to the right of opposing wrongdoing, to the
duty of fulfilling engagement, and to the friendship for one of two parties in
a state. (Hall Int. Law, page 261.)

Professor Pomeroy contends that it is impossible to place limita-
tions upon the question as to when intervention may or may not
be authorized. He insists that it is a branch of politics rather
than a subdivision of international law.

Henry Clay, while Secretary of State, wrote, May 10, 1825:

When the epoch of separation between a parent state and its colony, from
whatever cause, arises, the struggle for self-government on the one hand and
the preservation of power on the other produces mutual exasperation and
leads to a most embittered and ferocious war. It is then that it becomes the
duty of third powers to interpose their humane offices and calm the passions
and enlighten the councils of the parties.

The present Secretary of State, speaking in the Senate on the
28th of February, 1896, stated that if Spain continued Weyler's
policy the people of the United States would—

go over to that island and drive out these barbarous robbers and imitators
of the worst men who ever lived in the world. * * * We will not shield
ourselves behind the position taken by the British Government in the case
of Armenia, that Armenia was so far away and beyond her power that Great
Britain could not help those people when they were being murdered. * * *
But Cuba lies right at our door.

The words of Fish to Mr. Cushing, November 5, 1875, show that
the conditions then existing were deemed almost of sufficient
gravity to warrant intervention. He refers to the inhumanity
characterizing Spain's conduct in Cuba and the omission of the
Spanish Government to perform its treaty obligations to the
United States, and then states that—

It becomes a serious question how long such a condition of things can or
should be allowed to exist, and compels us to inquire whether the point has
not been reached where longer endurance ceases to be possible. * * * In
the absence of any prospects of a termination of the war or of any change in

the manner in which it has been conducted on either side, he (the President) feels that the time is at hand when it may be the duty of other governments to intervene, solely with a view of bringing to an end a disastrous and destructive conflict and restoring peace in the Island of Cuba.

The London Times, in an editorial January 26, 1876, discusses Spain's relations to Cuba and the letter of Secretary Fish just referred to, arraigning the Spanish-Cuban policy. In the editorial these words are used:

The purists of international law may at once be warned off the field of discussion. They may say that the United States has no more right to dictate how Spain shall govern than Spain has to order the reorganization of the South. * * * But these arguments are fit merely for lecture rooms. The practical answer is that the general rule of international usage conveniently called international law can be applied only to the ordinary cases of warfare. Since there is no international parliament, each nation is justified in defending its interest by exceptional measures when they are attacked in an exceptional manner. * * * We find, then, that Spain has driven one of the finest islands in the world into revolt; that she is trying to suppress the revolt by systematic savagery, and that the restoration of peace by mere force is all but hopeless. * * * Nor can we blame him (Mr. Fish) for insisting that if Spain shall not set Cuba free she is bound to make it orderly.

Messrs. Buchanan, Mason, and Soulé, in their joint dispatch to the Secretary of State October 18, 1854, declared that whenever Spain's possession of Cuba—

seriously endangered our internal peace, or the existence of the Union, the United States would be justified by human and divine law in wresting it from Spain.

President Grant contemplated intervention, as is evidenced by his message of 1874, wherein he says—

that the inability of Spain to suppress the insurrection may make some positive steps on the part of other powers a matter of self-necessity.

A similar statement occurs in his message the following year. Mr. Cleveland recognized that our obligations to Spain would not prevent us from intervening when it was manifest that "Spain's sovereignty was extinct in the island." Mr. McKinley recognizes that intervention with force is permissible "in the discharge of obligations to ourselves, to civilization, and humanity."

I have shown that Spain's savage and inhuman course, persistently pursued with respect to Cuba, justified the revolution, and that by every proper standard Spain's right to control Cuba has been forfeited. It has been shown that her desire to retain the island is purely mercenary; and that for three-quarters of a century the island has been the arena of insurrections, revolutions, and carnage, the direct and certain results of Spain's misconduct.

That during all of this time, by reason of the geographical situation of Cuba and the menace which her possession by an unfriendly power would be to our security and peace, and also because of our commercial relations with her, and the property rights which our citizens have acquired therein, as well as the desire which we entertain for the spread of republican institutions and the dedication of this continent to political freedom, we have regarded her with the utmost solicitude.

Attention has also been called to the Monroe doctrine, which devolves upon this nation the duty of preventing the acquisition of Cuba by any other nation; and the great trouble, complications, and expense occasioned this nation because of Spain's inability to preserve peace in the island; the irritation and trouble to the American people so great as to disturb their peace as a nation, and, in self-defense, to compel a change in the hitherto "expectant attitude of our Government."

3223

Attention has been directed to the views of jurists and the views of distinguished American statesmen in support of the proposition that forcible intervention in the affairs of another nation may be justified. With the facts before us, in the light of the century's events and the present tragic condition of the island, I ask can it be possible that there is any member of this House who denies the justification or the duty of the United States to immediately recognize the independence of the Cuban Republic and aid its armies, as the forces of England, France, and Russia supported the armies of Greece, in putting an end to the slaughter of innocents, the devastation of a country, and the commission of a crime against humanity?

In so doing we would also be defending American citizens now in Cuba, protecting their property, preserving our commerce, restoring peace to the nation, and performing such acts as the laws of self-defense and self-preservation impose upon every government. If Spain refuses to relinquish control of Cuba, it would mean war. In this programme territorial acquisition should not be considered. It is true that great statesmen like Jefferson, Adams, and Polk desired the annexation of Cuba, and unquestionably many of the inhabitants of Cuba desire to plant themselves under the flag of this great Republic.

But the forcible deprivation of a nation of any portion of its territory, with a design to make it a part of our national domain, is unwise, if not criminal. After Cuba's independence shall have been fully recognized, after the billows of war shall have lost themselves in the calm of peace and rest, after the shock of this terrible conflict shall have been forgotten and the cool, dispassionate judgment of the Cuban people shall have been consulted, after the people of this broad land have evidences of the fruits of independence in Cuba, after all of the mists and clouds and lurid flames that now encircle us have been cleared away, then if the people of Cuba earnestly desire to merge their future into ours it will be ample time to consider the question of annexation.

Will the Cuban people be capable of self-government? I have met many who entertain grave doubts. The stormy scenes in the Spanish-American Republics are referred to as examples of Cuban independence. It is true that Cuba will embark upon the career of free government under unauspicious circumstances; but I am persuaded that there is enough intelligence, virtue, integrity, and stability to be found among her people to give reasonable assurance of the permanency of the government agreed upon. Though the island is desolate, it is productive and fertile.

In 1887 there was a population of over 1,700,000. Perhaps when the present war began it had reached 2,000,000. Undoubtedly more than 500,000 have perished within the past three years, but there are brave and courageous men and women who will bring to the new and difficult problems high patriotism, singleness of purpose, and an unalterable determination that the fruits obtained by long years of suffering, of sorrow and tears and bloodshed shall not be lost. The negroes, numbering from 27 to 30 per cent of the population, are industrious, intelligent, and law abiding.

The Cuban people are different from those inhabiting the South American Republics. In the latter they are factional, emotional, the followers of men rather than the devotees of principle. Residents of the same State are not homogeneous. High mountains, wide rivers, and impenetrable forests separate communities, pro-

3223—4

duce provincialism, breed isolation, and subtract from national pride and prevent a love of national institutions.

In Cuba there is the utmost fraternity between Cubans and amity between races. There is no sectionalism. The railroads and the rapid ocean transportation bring the people together and produce harmonious thought and action. They are more conservative. more enlightened. more in harmony with the spirit and high impulses of the age than the people of South America. For years many of the young men and women have been receiving education in the United States.

Many have intermarried with Americans. Those who have returned have carried with them love of republican institutions and much of the genius of our institutions. At least 25,000 Cubans are now in the United States. With the advent of peace they would return and contribute materially in establishing order and founding a stable, liberal government.

The English language is not a stranger there. American interests are extensive, and with peace and stability assured, American capital would seek investment and thousands of our citizens, enticed by the beauty of the island, the fertility of the soil, and its incomparable climate, would there seek homes and add strength to its political, social, and economic superstructure. It has been charged that the insurgents will control the situation and organize a powerful military government, or produce a state of anarchy.

The personnel of the Cuban army disproves this statement. Patriots are its officers and they show no vaulting ambition. They long for peace and will gladly welcome the hour when they may return to the rebuilding of the devastated island.

Our duty is plain. The past and present, the martyred dead and sorrowful living, the voice of our country and the spirit of never-dying justice, command us to perform it.

Is true freedom but to break
Fetters for our own dear sake,
And with leathern hearts forget
That we owe mankind a debt?
No; true freedom is to share
All the chains our brothers wear,
And with heart and hand to be
Earnest to make others free.
They are slaves who dare not speak
For the fallen and the weak;
They are slaves who will not choose
Hatred, scoffing, and abuse,
Rather than in silence shrink
From the truths they needs must think.
They are slaves who dare not be
In the right with two or three.